Contents

CW00538631

Introduction

This course book is designed to provide you with the basic knowledge you need to identify and deal with hazards in the workplace, so that you can help to reduce accidents at work. It presents the core information required to achieve the NEBOSH Award in Health and Safety at Work, which is the perfect introductory qualification for those who need to understand the principles of health and safety as part of their job.

Whether you intend to work through this course book alone or are using it as part of a taught course, you should find that it contains the essential knowledge you need to prepare for the formal NEBOSH assessment. This takes the form of:

- a multiple-choice assessment; and
- a practical risk assessment activity, which is carried out in your own workplace.

The course book has been structured to match the NEBOSH syllabus, with the information divided into distinct elements, each of which starts with your learning outcomes for that particular section. If you have access to the Internet, we would recommend that you supplement this information by making use of additional resources, e.g. free leaflets from the UK Health and Safety Executive (available to download from www.hse.gov.uk) and guidance included on the International Labour Organisation's SafeWork website (www.ilo.org/safework). Other sources of information are available from the websites given in the References sections throughout.

We are going to cover lots of different aspects of health and safety at work, including ways to control common workplace hazards such as fire, manual handling, work equipment, hazardous substances and transport. When we talk about "health and safety at work" we need to consider the whole time a worker is "in the course of his/her employment". For example, working in an office, factory or shop is included and working in someone's home providing care is too. In addition, activities such as driving for work and working on another employer's premises are also covered.

Throughout the course book we will focus primarily on practical knowledge of health and safety which will be equally applicable to any type of workplace. As you work through, you will notice that the examples included relate to all sorts of industries, e.g. offices, manufacturing, and service industries such as care homes and catering, etc. You are also expected to apply the principles you learn to familiar situations in your own workplace.

The course book is intended to be suitable for those working in the UK and international students working all over the world. Generally, health and safety systems, controls and guidance which constitute best practice have been used as the basis, together with international standards and examples from the UK. Knowledge of specific legislation, either in the UK or in your own country, is not required and will not be included in the formal assessment.

We recommend that you spend a total of at least 24 hours studying for the NEBOSH Award in Health and Safety at Work; this includes four hours preparing for your practical risk assessment activity. Details of how to take the formal assessments can be found on the NEBOSH website www.nebosh.org.uk, where you will also find additional information including a syllabus summary.

A guide to the symbols used in this course book

PAUSE FOR THOUGHT/ACTIVITY
These ask you to think about what you have been learning, to relate it to your own experience, or to carry out an activity to reinforce what you have just read.

EXAMPLE
Real or imagined scenarios that give context to points made in the text.

Element 1   The foundations of health and safety

This element focuses on some initial concepts which are fundamental to this course book. You will become familiar with some of the meanings of common words used in health and safety and then look at the reasons why health and safety is important.

On completion of this element, you should be able to:

1.1 Outline the scope and nature of workplace health and safety

1.2 Identify the reasons for practising good standards of health and safety

1.3 Identify the key internal and external sources of health and safety information

The scope and nature of workplace health and safety

Before you read this section, pause to consider what 'health' and 'safety' mean to you. Then read on to learn what they mean in the context of this course book.

All subjects tend to use their own terminology and health and safety is no exception. Therefore, it is important that you understand from the beginning some of the most common terms used by health and safety professionals. These will be used throughout this course book.
It is important that you can appreciate both the meaning of these terms and the differences between them. These are not always obvious to people who are new to health and safety but don't worry, you'll soon be very familiar with them.

1. Health, safety and welfare

Health
The most common definition of *health* comes from the World Health Organisation, namely: "a state of complete physical, mental, and social well-being and not merely the absence of disease, or infirmity".

Health has a very wide meaning and does not just relate to whether you are free of a particular disease. It also takes into account other things such as how you feel both physically and emotionally about your health, how you live, how you interact with society, and the effect of the environment around you.

In relation to the definition of health we've just looked at, think about:

- the short-term and long-term health effects of drinking large amounts of alcohol;
- the effects on health of stress.

Can you now begin to see the wider meaning of the term "health"?

Throughout this course book we are only referring to health issues as they are affected by work. This is most commonly called 'occupational health'.

When used together, *health and safety* generally refers to all aspects of maintaining a healthy and a safe workplace where harm to people is prevented. This can include many issues such as laws, management systems and training, as well as physical items such as guards on dangerous machines.

Safety
Safety is not merely the absence of accidents, but the results of ALL persons taking positive actions to identify accident causes and implement suitable preventative measures.

The term "safety" tends to relate to physical dangers such as those from machinery or falling from a height.

Welfare
Welfare is the availability of facilities and presence of conditions required for reasonably comfortable, healthy, and secure living.

Welfare facilities which should be provided and maintained for workers include toilets, washing facilities, rest facilities and drinking water. Workers should use welfare facilities correctly and help the employer to keep them clean and well maintained.

2. Accident, dangerous occurrence, near-miss and work-related ill-health

Accident
An *accident* is any unplanned occurrence which results in some loss, often an injury.

An accident is always an unplanned occurrence. The most common kinds of accidents which occur in workplaces are slips, trips and falls; falls from height; being injured while carrying or moving objects; and being struck by moving or falling objects.

Dangerous occurrence

The International Labour Organisation (ILO) defines a *dangerous occurrence* as a "Readily identifiable event as defined under national laws and regulations, with potential to cause an injury or disease to persons at work or the public."

A dangerous occurrence is "any unplanned occurrence which normally results in some loss or damage to machinery and/or the workplace but has not resulted in injury."

Examples of things which might be classified as a dangerous occurrence include large scaffolding collapses, a crane overturning, and fires which stop normal activity for more than 24 hours in the workplace.

Near-miss

A *near-miss* is "an incident in which no injury or damage results."

Generally, workplace incidents are very much more likely to result in a near-miss than an actual injury. For every one injury there are probably at least another 90 near-misses. The important thing is to report and act on a near-miss so that action can be taken to ensure that it doesn't happen again. Next time the consequences could be far more serious. Near-miss reporting could help highlight some of the less obvious hazards in a workplace, or identify areas where a problem is developing.

Work-related ill-health

This is defined as "any physical or psychological ill-health which is caused by or affected by your work."

The most common types of work-related ill-health include:

- effects on muscles and bones of the upper limbs and back;
- work-related stress, which can be caused by many things such as poorly organised work, difficulties with colleagues, etc.;
- diseases caused by exposure to certain chemicals and other substances, e.g. detergents causing dermatitis and asbestos causing lung disease;
- hearing loss caused by long-term exposure to loud noises.

For this Activity you will need some index cards or pieces of paper.

Write each of the following terms on a separate card:

Health, Safety, Welfare, Accident, Dangerous Occurrence, Near-Miss, Work-Related Ill-Health

Then write each of the meanings given above on a separate card.

Mix all the cards up and then match the correct meaning to each term.

3. Health, safety and workplace fire law and guidance

Any country that has adopted International Labour Organisation Convention C155 "Occupational Safety and Health Convention, 1981" must have, in their own country, a system promoting health and safety which includes relevant laws.

In the UK, the laws which first started to regulate health and safety were first made many years ago. In certain industries, such as the manufacture and processing of cotton, these laws have been in place since the 1830's. These laws have changed a great deal over time and now the most important in England and Wales is the Health and Safety at Work, etc. Act 1974 (HSW Act 1974) which regulates general safety, health and welfare at work. This Act is quite general and gives very little actual detail on what should be done. The details are covered in legal Regulations and Orders; Approved Codes of Practice and Guidance.

Workplace fire safety is regulated in England and Wales through the Regulatory Reform (Fire Safety) Order 2005 and in Scotland through the Fire (Scotland) Act 2005.

Looking outside of the UK there are health and safety legal systems operating worldwide. Many of these follow the International Labour Organisation (ILO) model which requires employers to protect both workers and the public so far as is reasonably practicable. "Reasonably practicable" means that when deciding what to do to protect workers and others such as visitors, employers will be expected to do all that is possible or technically feasible to adequately control the risk, based on local or national legislative principles. Employers can balance the health and safety risk of an activity against the cost (in terms of money, time or effort needed) of controlling this risk. Here, for protection to be "reasonably practicable" the risk and the cost should be balanced, therefore a high risk might require more resources to adequately control it than would a low risk.

The specific situation in your country may vary but generally health and safety laws apply to all businesses, however small, including the self-employed and to workers.

4. Health, safety and workplace fire enforcing agencies and inspectors

Where any laws exist, it is important that they are enforced by an independent regulator if they are going to be effective. There should also be adequate penalties if the laws are violated. The system of enforcement varies significantly around the world but is most often carried out by Labour Inspectors or in the case of the UK by Health and Safety Inspectors from either the Health and Safety Executive (HSE) or the Local Authority. The Health and Safety Executive enforces health and safety at factories, farms and building sites, while the Local Authorities have enforcement powers in offices, shops, hotels and catering, and leisure activities. Workplace fire safety in the UK is generally regulated by the Fire Authority.

The range of powers that these Inspectors have varies, but most commonly:

- they can enter any premises;
- they will inspect workplaces to check that people are obeying the rules as laid down by law and give advice;
- they can take samples or look at records;
- they can interview any persons;
- they may investigate accidents and complaints.

When they find things that are seriously wrong, Inspectors may take enforcement action. This enforcement action might require specific improvements to be made in a set time, in which case the Inspector in the UK will issue an Improvement Notice. However, the issue may be so serious that the Inspector requires some or all work to stop until the necessary action has been taken to make the situation safe. In this case a Prohibition Notice will be issued. In the most serious circumstances the ultimate sanction for an enforcing agency will be to prosecute a company and/or individual workers. Such a decision is not taken lightly.

The reasons for practising good standards of health and safety

Before you read this section, note down some reasons why you think health and safety is important.

We will come back to these later.

There are a number of very important reasons why organisations and workers should see health and safety as a priority. For ease of understanding, these reasons have been grouped under three main headings:

- Moral;
- Legal;
- Financial.

1. The moral reasons

Very few if any organisations deliberately set out to allow their workers to be injured through their work. Most organisations and the people who work for them try to do what they believe to be the right thing. Some people call this moral. Others call it ethical or humanitarian.

Many people across the world are killed or seriously injured at work each year. In 2005, the International Labour Organisation (ILO) estimated that there may be as many as 2.2 million people dying each year as a result of work-related accidents and diseases[1]. This number exceeds the average annual deaths from road accidents, war and HIV/AIDS combined.

In the UK alone, from April 2009 to March 2010[2]:

- 152 people were killed as a result of work;
- nearly a quarter of a million other injuries are believed to have occurred; and
- 1.3 million people believed they were suffering from an illness which was caused or made worse by their current or past work.

These figures do not show the pain and suffering caused to the individuals concerned and the effects on their families and friends resulting from these occurrences.

The good news is that many if not all of these injuries and diseases are preventable. The numbers injured have reduced significantly in the last 30 years, mainly as a result of better health and safety standards.

2. The legal reasons

Many countries of the world have laws to ensure that employers do as much as they can to prevent people being injured as a result of their work. These laws are also there to protect the general public from workplace dangers. Obviously, organisations wish to avoid prosecution, since they could be fined, they would receive bad publicity and, most seriously, individuals within their organisation could go to prison.

The reasons for practising good standards of health and safety

3. The financial reasons

Before you read this subsection, consider what sort of financial costs a company might incur as a result of having poor health and safety standards.

We will come back to the things you've thought of later.

Good health and safety practice is also good business. Accidents and ill-health at work cost money. The Health and Safety Executive estimates that in the UK alone 23.4 million working days are lost due to work-related ill-health and 5.1 million due to workplace injury[2]. Spending money on health and safety before accidents occur will result in much bigger savings later on.

Costs to the business of accidents and ill-health may be felt straight away, including such things as:

- sick pay for an injured worker;
- accident investigation costs;
- associated repairs action;
- lost productivity;
- costs for additional workers to make up for loss of productivity;
- action which may be necessary to put right the health and safety problem.

EXAMPLE
The cost of accidents – the Buncefield oil storage depot incident December 11 2005

On the morning of December 11 2005, a leak from a storage tank resulted in a very large explosion and fire at a storage depot at Buncefield in Hertfordshire in the UK. The depot, which supplied aviation fuel to Heathrow and Gatwick airports as well as fuels to other users, was operated by five companies. Fortunately, nobody was killed in the accident although 43 workers were injured. The cost of rebuilding the storage facility was estimated at £70 million. The five companies had to pay fines and court costs of almost £10 million and two of the companies went into liquidation.

However, in addition to these costs the report on the incident suggested that the companies would be liable to costs of nearly £900 million arising from the accident. This sum was made up of:

- Claims for damages of £625 million from over 740 other firms operating in and around the site, from over 3,000 local residents, and from 7 local authorities.
- Costs of £245 million from airlines because of the disruption to fuel supplies.
- Costs of £15 million from government agencies for work arising from the investigation.
- £7 million for the cost of emergency response.
- £2 million for the environmental damage to the water supply in the area.

In addition there were unquantifiable costs caused by disruption to businesses operating in the area (including the administration of the London congestion charge, medical and public service records) and the temporary closure of the M1, M10 and M25 motorways.

Other much larger costs will probably be felt later and might include increased insurance premiums and fines associated with any prosecution. The Health and Safety Executive in the UK has estimated that this "hidden" cost can be as much as 8 to 36 times larger[3].

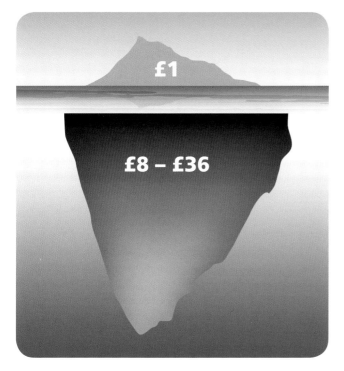

The hidden costs of accidents

It may be possible to insure against some of these costs, but others like lost time and sick pay will not be part of any insurance. Other negative effects on the organisation may not necessarily be seen directly as an immediate loss of money. These changes tend to be more subtle and include loss of a company's reputation with customers, possibly resulting in loss of contracts; poor publicity; and increased concern from the public.

Examples of financial costs	Examples of non-financial costs
Sick pay	Reputation with customers
Lost time	Reputation with neighbours
Damages and repairs	Poor staff morale
Fines and legal costs	Bad publicity
Accident investigation costs	People being less likely to want to work for an organisation
Increased insurance premiums and compensation to victims	

Return to the financial costs you considered at the beginning of this subsection.

Can you see now the financial benefits of good health and safety practice?

EXAMPLE
It is very difficult to predict exactly what the costs of an accident will be, particularly the legal costs, but this fictitious example will give you an idea of what may be involved.

A worker has had an accident at work. He tripped over some boxes in a store room because the light in that area was not working correctly. The worker suffered a broken arm and was off work for four weeks. The organisation knew about the problem with the light but had left it because it was decided that it was too expensive to call out an electrician, who had quoted £150 to complete the repair. The organisation was prosecuted in court over the accident by the enforcing agency and was convicted. The total cost to the organisation of the accident was:

Action	Cost
Accident investigation costs by consultant	£500
Lost time and cost of agency worker to cover (4 weeks of 37 hours @ £8 per hour)	£1,184
Wage cost for the worker involved (4 weeks @ £400 per week)	£1,600
Repair costs to light after accident	£150
Legal costs	£1,000
Production loss costs	£1,200
Increased insurance premium	£500
Fine for accident	£3,000
Total cost	£9,134

So, instead of paying out £150 to have the light repaired when it failed, this broken light eventually cost the firm over £9,000, as well as the pain and suffering caused to the injured worker and the damage caused to the organisation's reputation when they were convicted in court.

1. At the beginning of this section you were asked to note down some reasons why health and safety is important. Return to them now and group them under the three categories of moral, legal and financial. (Issues like bad publicity or people being less likely to want to work for an organisation should be grouped under non-financial reasons.)

2. If you have access to the Internet, explore the Health and Safety Executive Better Business website at www.hse.gov.uk/betterbusiness/index.htm. Find three facts there which show that health and safety can save organisations money.

The sources of health and safety information

There are many sources of health and safety information which can help organisations meet their health and safety obligations. Some of these are internal to the organisation, while others may be external.

Examples include:

Internal

Written/printed
- Health and safety policy
- Health and safety posters
- Accident data and reports
- Risk assessments

Verbal
- Verbal instructions from supervisors or managers

Observational
- Results from internal audits and inspections possibly carried out by organisation's own management

External

Written/printed
- Legal and other guidance from bodies such as the enforcing agency, trade bodies, etc.
- Material safety data sheets
- Manufacturers' information

Verbal
- Verbal instructions from Health and Safety Inspectors

Observational
- Results from external audits and inspections possibly carried out by health and safety consultants

You will learn more about some of these sources of health and safety information later on.

References

1   www.ilo.org/global/About_the_ILO/Media_and_public_information/Press_releases/lang--en/WCMS_005176/index.htm
2   www.hse.gov.uk/statistics/index.htm
3   HSE INDG275
    Managing health and safety: Five steps to success (www.hse.gov.uk/pubns/indg275.pdf)

Practice Questions

Q1 Which is an internal source of information?
   A Accident and absence records
   B Information from enforcement agencies
   C Local legislation and standards
   D Manufacturers' data

Q2 Which is a moral reason for preventing accidents and ill-health in the workplace?
   A Prevention of lost production
   B To prevent pain and suffering
   C To prevent adverse publicity for the company
   D To prevent damage to plant and equipment

The responsibility for health and safety

This element focuses on how health and safety should be managed within an organisation. It discusses who has responsibilities for health and safety and what these responsibilities are. You will look at systems used to manage health and safety.

Learning outcomes

On completion of this element, you should be able to:

2.1 Outline the health and safety role and responsibilities of relevant parties
2.2 Outline the key features of a system to effectively manage health and safety
2.3 Outline how accidents are caused and the role and function of accident recording and investigation
2.4 Identify the methods of improving health and safety performance

The health and safety role and responsibilities of relevant parties

Before you read this section, consider your own responsibilities for health and safety. Do they just involve you as an individual or are you also responsible for managing staff?

1. Roles and responsibilities of people within an organisation

In all organisations some people will have greater responsibilities for health and safety than others. It is important that everyone, including the Managing Director, knows what their own responsibilities are.

Employers

The main responsibilities lie with the employer for the health, safety and welfare of workers and the health and safety of anyone else who is affected by their work activities (e.g. visitors, agency workers, contractors, the general public).

EXAMPLE

A company is carrying out roofing work on a shop building in a busy street. The company has a responsibility to ensure that its workers are safe, e.g. by providing roof edge protection to prevent workers falling from height. The company has an equal duty to ensure that people working in the shop or walking in the area below are not injured by the work taking place on the roof. This would include considering how to stop roof materials falling and hitting pedestrians below.

In the UK and within the many other health and safety legal systems which follow the International Labour Organisation (ILO) model operating worldwide, employers have a duty to protect both workers and the public so far as is reasonably practicable. As we said earlier, this simply means that when deciding what to do to protect workers and others (such as visitors), employers can balance the health and safety risk of an activity against the cost (in terms of money, time or effort needed) of controlling this risk. In any case, the risk must be adequately controlled.

Some workers within an organisation have specific health and safety responsibilities.

Directors

Health and safety should be seen as an important part of business activity and should be "led from the front" by the Board of Directors. Members of the Board and senior managers have both a collective and an individual responsibility for health and safety. If there are serious failures, then in UK law and in many other countries, individual senior company representatives can be prosecuted if they have been negligent. It is a good idea if one member of the Board is appointed as a "health and safety champion" with responsibility for the overseeing of company health and safety activities.

Health and safety should appear regularly on the agenda for Board meetings and progress against targets should be routinely monitored and reviewed. This might include items such as the scrutiny of health and safety performance, and a review of audit information. The most serious corporate risks should be reviewed by the Board.

The Board should also consider whether:

- adequate resources are allocated to health and safety;
- the organisation receives competent health and safety advice;
- serious or new risks have been assessed and controlled;
- workers or their representatives have been properly consulted on decisions that affect their health and safety.

The Board should also endorse and formally sign off the health and safety policy.[1]

The Director of a large engineering company was recorded as having said:

"Health and safety is as important to the Board as are the other three main areas of managing a company – finance, production and quality. Failure in any of these four areas can cost us the business."

Managers and supervisors

Managers and supervisors have the day-to-day responsibility for managing health and safety. This includes ensuring that the health and safety policy and controls identified through risk assessment are implemented.

They should make sure that:

- workers have received any necessary health and safety training;
- risk assessments are carried out and controls implemented;
- emergency procedures, such as fire evacuations, are obeyed;
- workers have been issued with and do wear the correct personal protective equipment; and
- safe working practices are followed.

Managers and supervisors may also carry out health and safety inspections and checks within their own work areas and in any other locations where workers are expected to work.

The degree of supervision necessary will depend a great deal on the level of risk, the complexity of the work and the competence of the workers. Younger and less experienced workers will need more supervision than those who are older and more experienced, but some degree of supervision will always be required.

Managers and supervisors should always set a good example. For instance, they cannot expect workers to wear any necessary personal protective equipment if they are not prepared to wear it themselves.

It is sometimes tempting to get the job done as quickly as possible even if doing so puts workers at greater risk. Where managers have been found to be negligent or have knowingly allowed unsafe practices, they can be prosecuted under UK law.

EXAMPLE

A worker of a company which processed upholstery for the automotive industry was injured on a machine which cut and moulded lengths of carpet. The machine operated by automatically pulling lengths of carpet from a roll and cutting them with a heated knife before moving them through to a heated press for moulding. The dangerous parts were protected by a fence which surrounded the whole of the machine. Access to these parts was gained, for example for maintenance, through doors which were fitted with electronic safety devices. The safety devices cut the power to the whole machine when the doors were opened. The machine had been suffering production problems for some time due to the carpet misfeeding into the machine and being cut to the wrong length. The manager had allowed the safety devices to be disabled so that the workers could go inside the fenced enclosure to adjust the carpet position manually while the machine was running. After a few weeks of this becoming "normal practice", one of the workers was accidentally entangled in the machine and badly injured. The manager, as well as the company, was successfully prosecuted.

Workers

Every worker has a responsibility to look after their own health and safety and that of any other person who might be affected by what they do or don't do. They should co-operate with their employer at all times on all issues of health and safety, e.g. always complying with safety notices and fire evacuations. Workers should use tools and other equipment correctly, and not interfere with or misuse equipment such as fire extinguishers provided for health and safety. Some workers may have other specific responsibilities, such as carrying out particular health and safety checks, e.g. that the local exhaust ventilation system (used to control dust and fumes in some industries) is working correctly.

The health and safety role and responsibilities of relevant parties

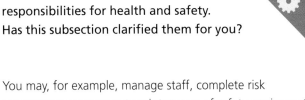

Now that you have read this subsection, come back to your own responsibilities for health and safety. Has this subsection clarified them for you?

You may, for example, manage staff, complete risk assessments or carry out maintenance of safety equipment. Whatever your responsibilities, it is important to understand that everyone has a general duty to look after their own health and safety; not to interfere with or misuse equipment provided for health and safety; and to co-operate with their employer.

2. Consultation

We have already mentioned that employers should consult with their workers on aspects of health and safety which affect them. The term "consultation" implies a constructive, two-way dialogue between workers and management. It allows workers to raise concerns, offer opinions and influence decisions. In small businesses, it may be possible to consult each worker separately. In larger organisations, workers can be consulted through health and safety representatives, who may be appointed by trade unions or "elected" by the workers themselves.

Consultation can be informal or formal, possibly through a health and safety committee which holds formal meetings usually between managers and appointed health and safety representatives.[2]

Typically these committees may:

- examine statistics on accident records and ill-health;
- review accident investigations and subsequent actions;
- discuss inspections of the workplace by enforcing authorities, management, or workers' health and safety representatives;
- review risk assessments;
- identify health and safety training needs;
- consider changes in the workplace affecting the health, safety and welfare of workers.

Benefits of consulting workers include:

- it is easier to identify risks and formulate joint solutions to problems;
- it shows workers that the organisation takes their health, safety and wellbeing seriously, and may improve morale;
- it should lead to greater awareness of health and safety among the workers and better control of workplace risks.

The benefits may not only be related to health and safety – businesses may also see improvements in overall quality and business efficiency.

Systems for managing health and safety

In the saying, "What is the best way to eat an elephant?", the answer is simple: "One bite at a time!"

A "system" is simply a way of managing something large or complicated by breaking it down into smaller, organised and logical stages.

1. Health and safety policy

Find a copy of your organisation's health and safety policy and keep it by you for reference as you study this subsection.

Alternatively, if you have access to the Internet there is a very simple example, freely downloadable at www.hse. gov.uk/risk/health-and-safety-policy-example.doc.

Effective health and safety management begins with the introduction of an effective health and safety policy. In UK law and good practice generally, organisations must produce a health and safety policy. The policy sets out the general vision, organisation and arrangements for the whole business. Again under UK law, if an organisation has five or more workers, the policy must be a written one. It is good practice to do this anyway. A health and safety policy may be a document that is required by an organisation's insurance company or a customer.

The UK Health and Safety Executive says that: "Your health and safety policy clearly sets out how you manage health and safety in your workplace by defining who does what; and when and how they do it".[3]

The detail of the information included within the policy will very much depend on the size and type of organisation to which it relates. A small administrative, office-based company will probably only require a very simple policy, but large companies or those with complex processes, such as those in the chemical industry, will require a far more detailed document.

Possible content of a simple policy may include details of:

- an overall statement publically declaring the directors' commitment to health and safety;
- how the company will prevent accidents and cases of work-related ill-health, and provide adequate control of health and safety risks arising from work activities; this may be achieved through risk assessment;
- a commitment to providing adequate training to ensure that workers are competent to do their work;
- arrangements for engaging and consulting with workers on day-to-day health and safety conditions and providing advice and supervision on occupational health;
- implementation of emergency procedures, e.g. the system for evacuation in case of fire or other significant incident;
- maintaining safe and healthy working conditions, providing and maintaining safe plant, equipment and machinery, and ensuring safe storage/use of substances;
- how health and safety information will be communicated to workers, e.g. in the UK by displaying the "Health and Safety Poster", and arrangements for consultation;
- first-aid arrangements and how accidents are reported and investigated; (perhaps in very small workplaces, where accident book(s) are located and accidents and ill-health at work are reported internally and if necessary to the enforcing authority).[3]

The health and safety policy should be signed off and authorised by the directors of the organisation and reviewed and revised on a regular basis as necessary.

Systems for managing health and safety

The modern equivalent of the Factories Act example we've just looked at would simply require the employer to ensure that the surfaces of the floors, walls and ceilings of all workplaces inside buildings are capable of being kept sufficiently clean. How the employer does this is left to them to decide. This type of law is now known as "goal setting".

3. Communication

For the health and safety policy to be implemented effectively, it must first be understood by all those it affects. The information it contains needs to be communicated accurately to all workers. However, effective communication is often cited by the regulators as the single most important area requiring improvement. Frequently the health and safety messages which managers and supervisors wish to give out are not the ones workers receive.

When planning on how to communicate with workers, the objective should be to present a clear and easily understandable message. The degree of complexity required will depend on who you are communicating with and what it is you are trying to communicate. In general, the degree of detail should be consistent with the level of complexity and the hazards and risks involved.

Probably the most common methods that organisations use to communicate with their workers are noticeboards, e-mails, intranet, health and safety manuals, posters, leaflets or health and safety newsletters. These are all techniques that can be successful when used to inform workers about health and safety issues.

However, these methods can sometimes be very "passive" and must be backed-up with more "active" methods such as toolbox talks (short presentations on a single aspect of health and safety), planned meetings, team briefings, etc. where workers can contribute and their level of understanding can be judged. Remember that managers and supervisors often communicate with workers verbally and may need to develop effective interpersonal skills.

There are some groups of workers with whom communication may present particular difficulties, such as those who work remotely from the main site, those who travel a great deal, or those who work from home.

2. Hazard identification, risk assessment and control

An effective health and safety management system has at its core a thorough but workable process for hazard identification, risk assessment and control. This will be discussed in more detail in the next element. Historical UK health and safety law was very specific, setting certain rules to control health and safety risks which often had to be followed exactly.

EXAMPLE

One example of this type of very "prescriptive" law was contained in the UK's Factories Act 1961. This required that factory walls with an impervious finish were to be "repainted in a prescribed manner or re-varnished at such intervals of not more than seven years as may be prescribed, and shall at least once in every period of fourteen months be washed with hot water and soap or other suitable detergent".

Clearly it is impossible for the law to cover every health and safety situation in every type of workplace. Risk assessment was developed to address this issue and is a technique which enables employers to look at the risks that arise in the workplace and then decide what sensible health and safety measures need to be put in place to control them.

There are different problems if workers have difficulty understanding the language spoken by the majority of workers, or if there are workers with low literacy levels. The aim of the organisation must be to ensure that these workers receive and understand the same information as all other workers. Managers may have to use interpreters or ask a work colleague to interpret for them; information may have to be translated (managers may have to check that this has been done properly); or the required information may have to be presented in a pictorial format, thereby reducing the reliance on written communication.[4]

Consider how effective the communication on health and safety is in your organisation. What could be done to improve it?

(You might consider toolbox talks, formal health and safety committees, etc.)

4. Monitoring and checking health and safety performance

You are probably already familiar with the need to monitor production levels, service provision or sales. Health and safety should be monitored in exactly the same way. Only by monitoring your current health and safety performance will you know what you need to do to improve.

Monitoring and measurement is a key step in any management process and forms the basis of continual improvement – the ongoing effort to improve products, services, processes or, in this case, health and safety. If measurement is not carried out correctly, there is no reliable information available for managers on how well the health and safety risks are being controlled.

To monitor health and safety performance effectively systems are needed which include techniques that provide feedback on performance *before* risks result in injury (e.g. surveys, inspections and audits), as well as those which give feedback on performance *after* incidents have occurred.

How accidents are caused

The main purpose of health and safety is to prevent death, injury and any illness occurring through work. One of the most important aspects of this is being able to understand how accidents which may lead to injury or illness may occur.

Accidents have an *immediate* cause, e.g. a worker tripping over a trailing electrical cable, but there will also be one or more *underlying* causes of why the accident occurred. In the case of the trailing cable, underlying causes may relate to why the cable was left trailing there (sometimes known as the *unsafe condition*) and why the worker did not see the cable and then tripped over it (sometimes known as the *unsafe act*).

The *root* cause of the accident is often the management failure from which all other failures stem. In the simple example we've just given this may be due to there being no system in place to deal with trailing cables, which may be a common situation throughout the workplace. Most, if not all, accidents can be prevented and the purpose of accident investigation is to discover the immediate, underlying and root causes in order to take action to prevent a reoccurrence. The results of the investigation, particularly the action taken, should be communicated to all concerned.

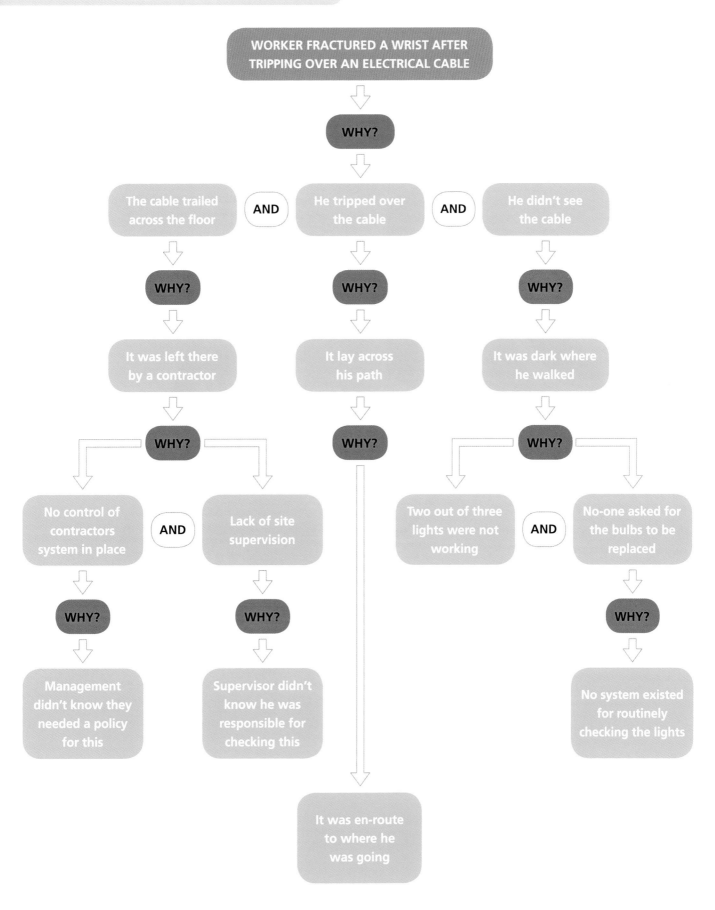

WORKER FRACTURED A WRIST AFTER TRIPPING OVER AN ELECTRICAL CABLE

WHY?

The cable trailed across the floor **AND** He tripped over the cable **AND** He didn't see the cable

WHY? WHY? WHY?

It was left there by a contractor

It lay across his path

It was dark where he walked

WHY? WHY? WHY?

No control of contractors system in place **AND** Lack of site supervision

Two out of three lights were not working **AND** No-one asked for the bulbs to be replaced

WHY? WHY? WHY?

Management didn't know they needed a policy for this

Supervisor didn't know he was responsible for checking this

It was en-route to where he was going

No system existed for routinely checking the lights

How accidents are caused

Accidents can often be seen as a chain of events and errors that lead almost inevitably to the final accident. This is sometimes described as the Domino Effect, where individual small errors all follow on in a sequence to cause the final outcome. By dealing with or removing one of these "dominos" the immediate accident will be prevented, but because the other dominos or causes still exist it is relatively easy for the sequence of events to reoccur. Getting to the root cause will eliminate the whole sequence.[5]

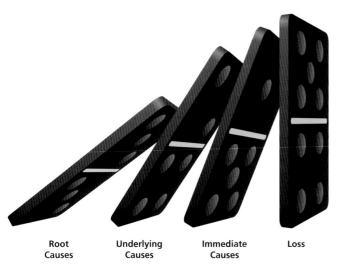

| Root Causes | Underlying Causes | Immediate Causes | Loss |

The Domino Effect

Consider an accident at work that you have been involved in or have witnessed. What do you think were the immediate, underlying and root causes?

If you have not experienced an accident, perhaps you can consider a "near-miss" – something that happened to you or you saw happen that COULD have led to injury? As above, consider the causes.

2. Accident and near-miss recording and reporting

The main role and function of accident and near-miss recording and reporting is to identify accidents so that they can be investigated and to prevent reoccurrence. Some of the more serious accidents may need to be reported to the enforcing authority. Workers should be encouraged to report all accidents to their line manager. Unfortunately many accidents and near-misses go unreported. Research has shown that an accident leading to injury is often preceded by many near-misses and that had these near-misses been reported and investigated, the injury could have been prevented.[6]

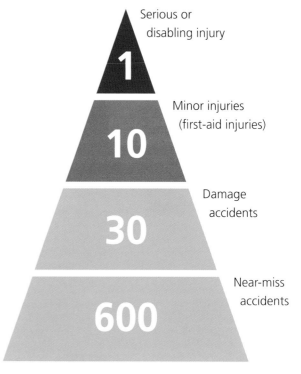

Serious or disabling injury

1

Minor injuries (first-aid injuries)

10

Damage accidents

30

Near-miss accidents

600

F.E. Bird's Accident Ratio Triangle

Managers should monitor near-miss, accident and ill-health information in order to identify any trends which exist. Organisations generally nominate a 'responsible person' to report accidents to the enforcing authority.

The purpose of the investigation is to discover the causes. This will enable management to put measures in place to prevent a recurrence of the accident. The purpose of an investigation is not to apportion blame.

Investigation is best done by a team of appropriately trained people, who may include a director or manager, the area supervisor, and safety representatives. Specialists, such as engineers, chemists or health and safety advisors, may also be needed.

The stages of an accident investigation

- *Taking charge of the immediate situation*
  - Make sure injured persons get immediate attention.
  - Secure the area of the incident.
  - Contain any hazards caused by the incident (switch off power; shut down machines).
  - Calm other people nearby.
  - Don't disturb the scene.
- *Gathering evidence*
  - Preserve evidence/take samples.
  - Take photographs/make sketches – record what you see.
  - Interview witnesses.
  - Interview the injured persons.
- *Assembly and analysis of the information*
  - Analyse information and determine the causes.
- *Implementation of findings*
  - Put measures in place to prevent it happening again.
  - Circulation of information to all relevant parties.

2.4 Improving health and safety performance

You have probably heard of the concept of continual improvement in relation to quality. This concept promotes a working culture where every worker is involved in improving business efficiency and performance. This is exactly what we are trying to achieve when we talk about improving health and safety and it is common to link quality and health and safety systems together.

How can you tell if your health and safety performance is good or bad? Examples of poor health and safety performance that you might look for include high accident rates, high absenteeism, unsafe behaviour, complaints, poor housekeeping and negative reports from health and safety advisors. Probably the best way to assess the situation is to use your eyes and ears and go out into the work area, where you are likely to see obvious examples of good or bad performance. These inspections or tours can be planned or ad-hoc. Note – inspections are planned and safety tours are not.

They can cover the whole site or operation or just be a snapshot of a particular department or process. Talk to workers about whether they feel health and safety on site is good or bad.

There are many factors which can have a negative effect on health and safety performance, such as:

- lack of resources;
- lack of management commitment;
- allowing unsafe behaviour to become the custom and practice;
- not understanding the risks involved in the job, possibly due to insufficient training and poor worker skills;
- lack of, or poor, risk assessment and control;
- ineffective communication.

Health and safety should be properly resourced but improving health and safety performance, and in particular promoting safer behaviour among workers, does not have to cost a lot of money. It does, however, require management commitment and one of the best ways to demonstrate this is through leadership by example. Organisations cannot expect workers to wear what may be uncomfortable personal protective equipment if the managers and supervisors will not do so themselves. Management should also chair meetings of the health and safety committee; be involved in investigations

of accidents, ill-health and incidents; and monitor performance regarding health and safety targets.

Specific action that the organisation will need to take will depend very much on what needs to be improved, but examples of things which commonly need addressing are:

- competence and training;
- promoting and if necessary enforcing safe behaviour;
- thorough risk assessment followed by implementation of any necessary actions;
- learning from past incidents;
- communication and consultation; and
- the regular monitoring of standards.

References

1   HSE INDG417 *Leading health and safety at work* (www.hse.gov.uk/pubns/indg417.pdf)
2   HSE INDG232(rev1) *Consulting employees on health and safety* (www.hse.gov.uk/pubns/indg232.pdf)
3   HSE INDG259(rev1) *An introduction to health and safety* (www.hse.gov.uk/pubns/indg259.pdf)
4   www.hse.gov.uk/involvement
5   HSE HSG245 (2nd ed.) *Investigating accidents and incidents* (www.hse.gov.uk/pubns/books/hsg245.htm)
6   HSE HSG65 (2nd ed.) *Successful health and safety management* (www.hse.gov.uk/pubns/books/hsg65.htm)

Practice Questions

Q3 Which is correct?

A The employer sets health and safety policy

B The worker interprets health and safety law

C The worker provides practical health and safety advice

D Workers have responsibility for establishing health and safety standards

Q4 When should the health and safety policy be communicated to workers?

A After an accident

B When a worker develops work-related hearing loss

C On induction and whenever changes have been made

D Every month

Q5 Which is an indicator of poor health and safety performance?

A Negative reports from workers

B Low accident rates

C Low levels of sickness absence

D Safe behaviour from workers

Q6 An example of an unsafe condition is:

A not wearing goggles to prevent an eye injury

B using a pedestal drill without a guard

C not wearing ear defenders to prevent hearing loss

D a trailing cable across a pedestrian walkway

Element 3 Health and safety risk assessment and control

This element focuses on hazards and risk, and in particular the need for and method of carrying out risk assessment. It discusses the principles of controlling exposure to health and safety risks and shows some common safety signs, identifying their type and purpose by the use of colours and symbols.

On completion of this element, you should be able to:

3.1   Outline the aim and objectives of risk assessment and give examples of common hazards

3.2   Explain what constitutes an adequate risk assessment

3.3   Outline the stages of risk assessment

3.4   Outline the general principles for controlling health and safety risks

3.5   Identify common safety signs

The aim and objectives of risk assessment

Risk is part of all of our lives. When we cross the road we make a judgment of whether or not it is safe to do so. We will consider in our heads such things as the speed and number of any approaching vehicles, how far it is to cross, the weather conditions, lighting, etc. before we make our decision to proceed. We might consider walking on a little further to a place where it is safer to cross, or we might use a pedestrian crossing if there is one nearby. The process that we go through in our head is a 'risk assessment'. We are going to apply the same principle to work. Employers need to consider whether they are doing enough to protect both workers and anyone else who might be affected by their work, e.g. visitors.

It is not possible to eliminate all risk, but employers are required to protect people "so far as is reasonably practicable", which you will remember we discussed in Element 1. We also said how risk assessment is a central part of the way that an organisation can effectively manage health and safety in Element 2.

Before we can examine how to do a risk assessment, you first need to understand the meaning of some common terms used in this element.

1. Meaning of hazard, risk and risk assessment

When thinking about a risk assessment, there are three common terms which are used which are very often confused. These are "hazard"; "risk"; and "risk assessment" itself.

Hazard

A *hazard* is "anything that might cause harm", such as trailing cables, electricity, working at height, etc. You should not wait for an accident to occur in order to look to identify hazards within your workplace. The Occupational Health and Safety Assessment Series (OHSAS) Standard, "Occupational health and safety management systems – Requirements", (OHSAS 18001:2007), states that you should aim to proactively identify all sources, situations or acts (or a combination of these), arising from the organisation's activities, with a potential for harm in terms of human injury or ill-health. Examples include:

- sources such as moving machinery, fire, noise;
- situations such as working at height or in confined spaces; and

- acts such as manual handling.

What are the most common types of hazard that exist in your workplace?

Which hazards do you think lead to the most accidents, both fatal and non-fatal?

Risk

A *risk* is the chance, large or small, that somebody (not necessarily a worker) could be harmed by hazards, together with an indication of how serious that harm might be. A more detailed definition is contained in OHSAS 18001:2007. This describes a risk as the combination of *likelihood* of an occurrence of a hazardous event or exposure(s) and the *severity* of injury or ill-health that can be caused by the event or exposure(s).

This is sometimes represented by the formula:

Risk = severity x likelihood

taking into account the number and type of people exposed.

Both severity and likelihood are discussed in more detail later in this element.

You should concentrate on the high risks. Very often straightforward and inexpensive things can be done to control risks; for example, removing trailing cables from a walkway. It is always better to avoid and remove risks if possible. An example would be cleaning windows from the ground using water-fed, extendable poles rather than working from ladders.

Risk assessment

The UK Health and Safety Executive says that *risk assessment* is "a careful examination of what in your work could cause harm to people, so that you can weigh up whether you have taken enough precautions to remove or control the risks or should do more to prevent harm".

Again OHSAS 18001 provides a more detailed definition where risk assessment is the "process of evaluating the risk(s) arising from a hazard(s), taking into account the adequacy of any existing controls, and deciding whether or not the risk(s) is acceptable".

There is no one "approved" method of risk assessment but throughout this course book we will be using the "5 steps to risk assessment" process developed in the UK by the Health and Safety Executive. This is suitable for low to medium risk situations.

The risk assessor makes an overall judgment of the level of risk, but this is a subjective view based on their own experience and the evidence they have gathered and examined. This is called a *qualitative* risk assessment.

If you work in a high hazard industry, like the chemical industry, you may come across other systems, possibly ones which use specific values to estimate overall risk severity, e.g. the probability of a particular pump within a chemical process failing. This is called *quantitative* risk assessment.

2. Common workplace hazards

Here are some examples of the most common workplace hazards that you are likely to encounter. The control of these hazards will be discussed in much more detail in subsequent elements.

Slips, trips and falls

These hazards are very common and are the most likely cause of workplace accidents, accounting for about one third of all major injuries. They can arise:

- from the physical nature of the floor surface;
- from sudden changes of level; and
- from substances like oil or obstructions such as boxes on the floor.

Falling objects

These might include:

- materials falling from work taking place overhead such as roof tiles, tools, etc. or;
- materials falling from racking or other storage areas.

Collision with objects

This includes walking or driving into fixed objects such as racking or the edge of machines.

Trapping/crushing under or between objects

All or part of the body may be trapped or crushed under or between objects. Examples include:

- boxes or pallets falling over;
- trapped fingers; or
- objects being worked on such as cars.

Manual handling

This involves the moving, lifting, carrying and manoeuvring of loads such as boxes or other people.

Contact with machinery/vehicles

This can involve direct contact with a dangerous machine or part of the clothing or body becoming entangled. Vehicle accidents account for a significant number of fatalities, particularly from reversing.

The aim and objectives of risk assessment

Electricity

Hazards come from contact with live parts but there are also supplementary hazards of fire, explosion and physical injuries, like falling and hitting the head when subject to an electric shock.

Hazardous substances

Hazards come from dusts like silica; gases like carbon monoxide; some chemicals; and biological organisms such as Legionella.

Fire and explosion

Fire and explosion hazard sources include gas cylinders, flammable liquids and dusts.

Psycho-social

An example of a psycho-social hazard is work-related stress.

Noise

Noise from equipment and plant can not only damage hearing but can also interfere with your ability to communicate effectively with other workers.

Vibration

Vibration can occur:

- to both the hands and arms when holding vibrating tools and equipment; or
- in some cases to the whole body, e.g. when driving off-road vehicles like tractors.

In the UK in 2009/10 the most common causes of fatal accidents based on total number reported were:[1]

Falls from a height (irrespective of height)	22
Struck by moving, flying or falling object	19
Struck by a moving vehicle	17
Trapped by something collapsing/overturning	11
Contact with moving machinery	10

Again in the same year the most likely causes based on total number reported of non-fatal major injuries to workers were:

Falls and slips combined	14,761
Slips, trips or falls on the same level	10,561
Falls from a height (irrespective of height)	4,200
Injured while handling, lifting or carrying	3,239
Struck by a moving, flying or falling object	2,810

Earlier in this element you were asked to think about the types of hazard which are most common in your workplace and which of them might lead to the most accidents, both fatal and non-fatal.

You can now compare the common types of hazard in your workplace with the common hazards listed above.

How does your thinking about the hazards likely to lead to fatal and non-fatal accidents compare with the statistics we've just looked at?

3. Aim and objectives of risk assessment

Once a hazard has been identified, possibly from an accident occurring or a problem being reported by a worker, the risk assessor has to make a judgment of what is the most likely outcome. To do this the risk assessor must make an estimate of the chance of the unintended incident occurring (the *likelihood*) and if the incident did occur what would be the *harm* caused. Many different systems to estimate both harm and likelihood are used.

Harm/severity

Many systems of categorisation are used. Some systems use a scale from slight or minor harm like a cut finger at one extreme right up to severe injury, permanent disability and death at the other, e.g. a fall from height of over 2 m could result in death.

Likelihood

The model we will be using as described earlier is the qualitative approach which uses words instead of absolute values/figures. In this case we say the likelihood of an outcome is, for example, "highly unlikely"; "unlikely"; or "likely" (originally from BS 8800/BS 18004).

It is important that the actions that need to be taken following a risk assessment are prioritised based on the relative level of risk. The highest risk issues should receive the most attention. Some risk assessment systems use the "*Risk = severity x likelihood*" concept as a way to prioritise or 'rank' risk in order of importance. This can be useful to help you prioritise the order in which risks should be dealt with. The problem is that this ranking can only ever be subjective and sometimes issues which are viewed as having the potential to occur very rarely can be ignored, although if they did occur their consequences could be serious. There is an equal possibility that issues which are perceived as having a low potential consequence are ignored even though dealing with them could be very straightforward.

Adequate risk assessment

The problem with risk assessment is that of judging the likelihood of the risk occurring and the harm that could occur – subjectivity is involved.

Poor risk assessment will result in inappropriate controls being put in place, which could even make an accident more likely to occur.

The important thing for any organisation is to understand how risk assessment can be improved. To do this it is useful to have these key questions in mind:

Who should be responsible for the risk assessment?

The employer has the overall responsibility to ensure that risk assessment is undertaken. This responsibility may be delegated to a manager to ensure that assessments are undertaken in his or her department. This is satisfactory providing the manager has the power to do something about any issues identified by the risk assessment. There must also be a clear reporting structure back to senior management to report on progress and on any important findings, particularly if they raise significant resource issues or have implications across the whole of the organisation.

Who should undertake the risk assessment?

The risk assessment should be undertaken by someone with the competence to do so. They must:

- understand enough about the work to identify the hazards involved;
- be able to assess the risk; and
- be able to identify existing controls and any further controls needed.

If an organisation does not feel it has anyone capable of doing this then it must get help from a competent source.

Who should be involved in the risk assessment process?

Those who are exposed to the risk, especially the workers most directly affected, should be involved in the risk assessment. They are likely to know far more about the process or situation which gives rise to the risk than anyone else. The workers may have noticed things that are not immediately obvious to the assessor. They may have already developed their own solutions to protect themselves from the risk, which the risk assessor can consider. Where available, health and safety representatives should also be consulted and involved in the risk assessment process.

Does it meet legal requirements if relevant?

The purpose of the risk assessment from a legal point of view is to help determine what measures should be taken to comply with any health and safety law that might apply.

Does it identify all significant hazards?

There is plenty of help available in order to assist an assessor in identifying the hazards. We have already mentioned involving the workers, but other sources of information he or she may find useful include:

- relevant legislation and appropriate guidance, providing that it is from an "authoritative source";
- manuals produced by equipment or material manufacturers and suppliers; and
- information from trade associations, insurance companies, etc.

Is it current?

Employers must ensure that their risk assessments are up-to-date. This will probably mean that they are reviewed on a frequent basis, for example annually, to see if they are still valid, and revised if necessary. This may be a brief review to ensure that nothing has changed within the last 12 months which would mean that the assessment might be out-of-date, e.g. the same machine is still used in the same manner to produce the same product. An assessment should be undertaken before any new work commences or when a significant change has occurred.

Does it identify all people who may be affected?

All aspects of the work activity must be assessed, including both routine activities and any non-routine work such as cleaning and maintenance. The assessment must identify everyone who may be at risk from the work activity including visitors and, where appropriate, members of the public.

EXAMPLE

A risk assessment for roofwork undertaken in a public area such as a busy street would not only cover the workers on the roof but also members of the public who may be passing below, anyone working in the building itself and visitors who may need to examine the work such as architects, building inspectors, etc.

A risk assessment should cover such situations as mobile and off-site working, contractors and agency workers. It is also important that any particularly "vulnerable" people who may be more affected by the risk than others are

identified. This will largely be determined by the risk itself, but could include young workers (due to their age and lack of experience); pregnant workers; and those with a disability.

Once the risks are assessed, insignificant risks can usually be ignored.

Does it record all significant findings?

The risk assessor should record the "significant findings" from the assessment and it is important that these are effectively communicated to anyone who may be affected by the work.

In UK law the "significant findings" of the risk assessment should be written down if the organisation employs five or more people. As we saw with health and safety policies in Element 2, it is good practice to do this anyway as you may be required to produce it to an insurance company or a customer.

Management must ensure that any necessary actions identified from the assessment are undertaken as soon as practicable – this is very important. The UK Health and Safety Executive further advises that a risk assessment record should show that:

- a proper check of the hazards was made;
- those who might be affected have been identified;
- the employer dealt with all the obvious significant hazards, taking into account the number of people who could be involved; and
- the precautions are reasonable, and the remaining risk is low.

Adequate risk assessment

Is there a need to undertake "general" and "specific" risk assessments?

In some situations the general risk assessment we have discussed here is not the most suitable type of risk assessment to undertake. Some legal requirements, if applicable, are much more specific and require an employer to carry out a particular type of assessment for specific groups of workers.

EXAMPLE

In the UK, if workers are believed to be exposed to noise levels of 80 dB(A) or more (being a lower action level of a daily or weekly exposure to noise), an employer must assess the risk, to identify the necessary precautions needed to protect workers from that noise. If exposure is above 85 dB(A) (the second action level) the assessment should include formal measurement of noise in the workplace.

You will learn more about noise assessment and control in Element 10.

Other examples of situations where more "specific" risk assessments are undertaken include for:

- exposure to hazardous substances;
- exposure to vibration;
- manual handling activities; and
- use of display screen equipment.

Risk assessment should be "suitable and sufficient" or in other words adequate. In deciding the amount of effort an employer needs to put into assessing risks, you have to consider how significant the hazards are and whether precautions are in place so that the risks are small. Generally the more significant a hazard is, the more resources you should put into the assessment. For example, the amount of effort needed to assess the risks will be much greater in a chemical factory as compared to an ordinary office and the level of detail in the risk assessment will be much higher.

The stages of risk assessment based on the UK Health and Safety Executive's 5 steps

The stages of the 5-step approach are:

1. identify the hazards;
2. decide who might be harmed and how;
3. evaluate the risks and decide on precautions, applying controls to specified hazards;
4. record the findings and implement them;
5. review the risk assessment.

To help you carry out the risk assessment later, we will look in a little more depth at these "5-Steps":

*   *Identify the hazards*
    Walk around your workplace and look for those things in the workplace or activities that people are carrying out that can cause harm, such as electricity, chemicals, working at height, manual handling, dangerous machinery, noise, etc. Ask the workers and their representatives for their ideas on what can cause harm. A look at the accident book might be worthwhile too.

*   *Decide who might be harmed and how*
    Look for types of people (e.g. fitters, roofers, electricians, office workers) and others such as passers-by, visitors, security guards, etc. Try to think HOW they can be harmed – in other words, what type of injury could occur. Office workers may suffer eye-strain from using computers; roofers may fall from height; and security guards may face violence and aggression. Fitters could be drawn into dangerous machinery and crushed.

*   *Evaluate the risks and decide on precautions*
    This requires you to look for and understand the precautions that are in place already. For instance, the roofer may have handrails and walkways to stop him falling through or off the roof. He will wear safety boots and a helmet. But will that be enough? We now think of further precautions that will make his work even safer: we can use fall restraint that will stop him falling off – or fall arrest to catch him if he does. The fall arrest could be a harness, or airbags/nets.

*   *Record the findings and implement them*
    This means writing down the risk assessment, either on a paper form or into a computer database, whichever is more appropriate. You will show what you think can cause harm, who it can affect (and how) and what precautions are there/what more are needed. Implementation is about making sure the extra precautions are put in place. Prioritise by tackling the higher risks first, and tick them off as they are completed.

*   *Review the risk assessment*
    Things are likely to change, so you need to look regularly at the work to make sure what you have already done actually works, and that new hazards have not been introduced. You can decide a date to review, but if things happen in the meantime – such as a new machine, an accident, etc. – don't wait – review as it happens.[2]

The stages of risk assessment based on the UK Health and Safety Executive's 5 steps

This is the form you will be using in your Risk Assessment Activity for Unit HSW2:

WORKPLACE RISK ASSESSMENT

nebosh

Area/Unit/Department:		Completed by:		Review date:	
Activity:				Date:	
Hazards	Who might be harmed and how?	What is already being done to control the risk?	Are further controls needed?	Additional Actions	Priority

NB: This is for educational purposes only

3.4 Controlling health and safety risks

1. General principles

As a general principle, risks should be avoided altogether if this is possible. This statement is not advocating a 'risk-averse' world where no-one is allowed to do anything just in case they might be injured. It is, though, advocating a sensible approach to risk. Employers should consider whether work can be done in a different way, taking care to eliminate risk where possible and not to introduce any new hazards if possible.

When risks cannot be avoided, the risk assessment that we have discussed above should be carried out to determine what controls should be introduced. It is always better to deal with a risk at source, e.g. replacing broken flooring tiles is much better than informing staff of a potential tripping hazard.

Whatever measures are adopted to minimise risk, you should always consider the needs of individual workers. For instance, if safer working practices need to be designed for a new process, workers should be involved in the design and employers should always take advantage of any new technological advances, e.g. the development of safer machines. That said, it is always best to consider giving priority to those measures which protect the majority of the workforce.

2. General hierarchy of control

When determining whether risk controls are adequate or whether further measures are needed, consideration should be given to reducing the risks according to the following hierarchy. This hierarchy implies that it is much better to control risk through measures listed at the top of the hierarchy (elimination) than by relying on those at the bottom (personal protective equipment (PPE)). Only if it is found not to be practicable to control risk by elimination should you then move to the next one in the hierarchy, and so on until the only option that may be left to you is to consider PPE.

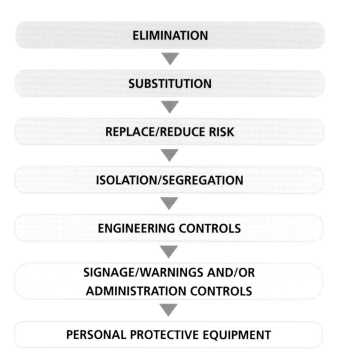

1. Elimination/substitution – get rid of the hazard altogether. If you can't, try replacing the hazardous with the less hazardous or non-hazardous, e.g. replacing a paint-spraying process with dipping; or replacing paints which contain ingredients which can cause asthma with those which don't; or removing solvent-based paint and using water-based paint instead.

2. Replace or reduce risk – possibly by limiting the time that workers are exposed to a risk, perhaps using job rotation. This is only possible with certain types of risk when it can be determined that the length of exposure is key to the risk, like high noise levels. Remember it is not acceptable to expose workers to very high-risk jobs like confined space entry, even for a short time, without taking the proper precautions.

3. Isolation/segregation of a risk from those affected
– e.g. by barriers or shields. Again this is very common in the control of noise. Noise enclosures which have limited entry, possibly only for the operator, are built around noisy machines. They significantly reduce the exposure for the rest of the workforce. Another example would include putting physical barriers between pedestrians and traffic such as fork-lift trucks.

4. Engineering controls – which might include specific types of guards on the dangerous parts of machinery, or local exhaust ventilation systems which remove contaminants like wood dust in a carpentry shop from the air.

5. Safe systems of work – a very common method used to protect against risk is by developing a safe method of working. This is particularly useful in combination with other methods such as engineering controls. For example, no matter how well a woodworking machine is guarded, if a process has to be used which cannot be automated, at some time the operator may come close to the blade or cutter. Safe systems of work which involve adopting the safest method to do the job can be very effective, e.g. the use of push-sticks, jigs and holders where the hands are kept away from the saw blade. The problem with this is that employers must rely on individuals to adopt these safe working methods. In this case the training, clear work instructions and the competence of workers, together with effective supervision, are crucial. Generally the more formal the safe system of work, the better it works. In high or unusual risk situations, formal written systems called "permits to work" are adopted. These describe both the hazards and precautions required in some depth. They follow a task through all of its stages and ensure safety by continuous monitoring up to and at the completion of the task.

6. Information, instruction, training and supervision – we have already mentioned the need for this when discussing safe systems of work above. Generally the better the level of information, instruction and training in a workplace accompanied by effective supervision, the safer the workplace will be.

7. Personal protective equipment (PPE) – if risk cannot be reduced to an acceptable level in any other way then employers will have to provide PPE like gloves, safety footwear, head protection and respiratory protection. This can be very effective for some risks such as objects falling onto the head and feet, providing the objects are not too heavy and they don't fall too far; and when handling equipment or material with sharp edges, etc. Unfortunately PPE is normally the first thing employers consider when trying to control risk rather than the last.

Management should not forget that adequate welfare arrangements such as washing facilities are also an important part of protecting against risk.

EXAMPLE
When workers are handling hazardous substances like lead, it is important that they can wash their hands before eating, as one of the main routes by which lead can enter the body is through ingestion.

3. The role of monitoring and health surveillance

It is important that, once control measures have been put in place, both workers and management monitor that they are working correctly and that they do not deteriorate or stop being used over time.

Health surveillance is a technique whereby management can monitor the health of individual workers to find out whether controls are effective by looking out for early signs of work-related ill-health. One of the most common types of health surveillance is audiometry, where workers' hearing is checked on a regular basis to see that it has not deteriorated and to ensure that noise controls are effective.

For practice, let us look, section by section, at a risk assessment, using the form you will be given by your training provider for your Risk Assessment Activity. One item will be completed for you as an example – can you fill in three more items yourself, completing all the columns in the assessment form?

PARTS 1 AND 2: THE HAZARDS AND WHO MIGHT BE HARMED
AREA/UNIT/DEPARTMENT: Main office, first floor
ACTIVITY: Office work (accounts, sending/receiving orders, printing leaflets)

HAZARDS	WHO MIGHT BE HARMED AND HOW
1. Use of printers to make leaflets: Electrical hazards of the printers. Hazardous substances (toner/ink cartridges). Noise when printers operate.	All office staff using the printers – electric shock. All staff – exposed to noise. Staff changing cartridges – exposed to toner and ink from spills. Other workers who may use the printers (unauthorised).
2. (insert appropriate hazard)	(insert who/how)
3. (insert appropriate hazard)	(insert who/how)
4. (insert appropriate hazard)	(insert who/how)

PARTS 3 AND 4: THE CONTROL MEASURES

WHAT IS ALREADY BEING DONE TO CONTROL THE RISK?	ARE FURTHER CONTROLS NEEDED?
Only trained, authorised staff use the printers. Only trained staff change ink or toner cartridges. Only one printer at a time runs to reduce noise. All printers are visually checked by users and formal annual examination and tests carried out (PAT).	Enforce checking that only authorised, trained persons use the printers. Fit noise-reducing containment hoods so all printers can operate at same time.
(insert what is being done)	(insert further controls)
(insert what is being done)	(insert further controls)
(insert what is being done)	(insert further controls)

PARTS 5 AND 6: ADDITIONAL ACTIONS AND PRIORITIES

ADDITIONAL ACTIONS	PRIORITY
Office supervision to make sure only authorised persons use the printers. Office supervision to ensure hoods are kept on when printers are running. Ensure Portable Appliance Testing (PAT) is carried out if any new printers introduced.	(low) (high) (medium)
(insert additional actions)	(prioritise)
(insert additional actions)	(prioritise)
(insert additional actions)	(prioritise)

Common safety signs

Sometimes where risk can't be avoided and even though controls have been put in place to reduce the risk, it may still be necessary to warn workers and others of any risk which exists. Safety signs provide a clear warning or sometimes give advice. They should be displayed in a prominent location close to the hazard. The pictograms should clearly display the meaning of the sign so wording is optional on signs.

Specific designs for safety signs are used in many countries for specific situations.

Prohibition signs

These are used to stop dangerous behaviour. They are round with a black pictogram on a white background, with red edging and a diagonal line.

No access for pedestrians sign

Warning signs

These signs give warning of a hazard or danger (e.g. "Danger: Men at work"). Warning signs are triangular with a black pictogram on a yellow background, with black edging.

DANGER: Men at work sign

Mandatory signs

These signs require specific behaviour; for example, "Ear protection must be worn". They are round, with a white pictogram on a blue background.

Ear protection must be worn sign

Emergency escape or first-aid signs (safe condition signs)

These signs give information on emergency exits/escape routes, first-aid, or rescue facilities. They are rectangular or square with a white pictogram on a green background.

First-aid sign

Fire-fighting signs

These are used to identify fire-fighting equipment and to mark permanently its location. They are rectangular or square shape with a white pictogram on a red background.

Fire extinguisher sign

References/Practice Questions

References

1   www.hse.gov.uk/statistics
2   HSE INDG163(rev2) *Five steps to risk assessment* (www.hse.gov.uk/pubns/indg163.pdf)

Practice Questions

Q7   Which is a hazard?
A   Back pain
B   Burns
C   Collision with objects
D   Dermatitis

Q8   Which is a hazard?
A   Hearing loss
B   Heat stroke
C   Noise
D   Sunburn

Q9   Which is correct?
A   Hazard identification should only be carried out by a manager
B   Safety inspections can be used to identify hazards in the workplace
C   There is only one way to identify hazards in the workplace
D   Workers should not be involved in hazard identification

Q10   The hierarchy of risk control places elimination at the top of the hierarchy. Which is an example of this?
A   Replacing a chemical with a less hazardous one
B   Reducing the weight of objects
C   Staff rotation
D   Not using pesticides

Q11   Which is correct?
A   If possible risks should be avoided altogether
B   Individual needs of workers do not need to be considered in risk assessment
C   Risk controls are only needed if there is a high level of risk
D   Risk control measures which protect most of the workforce do not need to be considered

Q12   Which shape and colour of sign would show that smoking is NOT permitted?
A   Blue, white and round
B   Black, yellow and triangular
C   Red, white and round
D   Green, white and rectangular

Element 4

Hazards and controls associated with work equipment

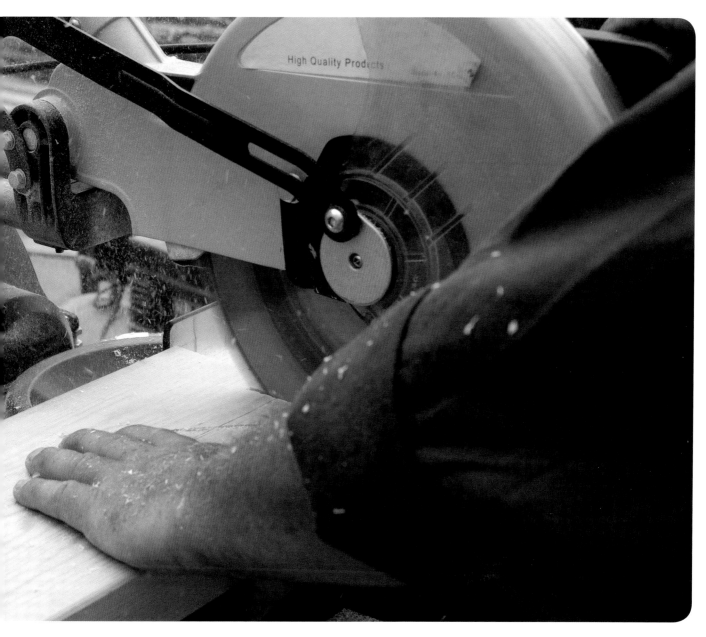

This element focuses on the health and safety hazards and controls associated with the tools, machinery and access equipment (e.g. ladders) that you use at work. This is collectively known as "work equipment".

Learning outcomes

On completion of this element, you should be able to:

4.1 Identify the general health and safety requirements for work equipment

4.2 Identify the main hazards and controls for work equipment

The general requirements for work equipment

The term "work equipment" refers to any equipment which you use in connection with your work. Common examples would include knives, photocopiers, ladders, and screwdrivers.

Note down some of the most common types of work equipment used in your workplace.

We will return to these later.

The scope of the term "work equipment" is very wide and for ease of understanding we can group work equipment into four main areas – hand tools, power tools, machinery, and access equipment. Vehicles which you may use at work are also work equipment, but because of the specific issues associated with them, we deal with them in a separate element (Element 5).

Hand tools

These are tools which are held and used by hand. They include such things as knives, hammers, hand-drills, screwdrivers, etc.

Power tools

Here we are referring to hand-held tools which are powered in some way – most often in a domestic setting by mains voltage (230V) electricity. At work other sources of power such as low voltage (110V) electricity, battery power, or compressed air may be used.

Machinery

A machine is a piece of equipment which has moving parts and is powered in some way. Here we are referring to machines which are not hand-held. They include such things as bench-mounted drills, paper shredders and photocopiers.

Access equipment

This is equipment which allows workers to access work areas which are not normally accessible. It is most often associated with working at height, although it can include other environments such as across water. It includes equipment like ladders, scaffolding and mobile elevated work platforms (MEWPs).

Using a 'cherry picker' for access at height

Earlier you were asked to note down some common work equipment used in your workplace. Return to your list now and group the items under the four types we've identified, i.e. hand tools, power tools, machinery, and access equipment.

Later in this element we will discuss in detail the hazards associated with each type of work equipment, as well as the ways in which the risks from them can be reduced. First though you need to understand what the main health and safety issues are which apply to all work equipment.

Employers should ensure that risks, created by the use of work equipment, are eliminated where possible or adequately controlled. The UK Health and Safety Executive further classifies these controls into:

- *'hardware' measures* – physical controls such as guards and protective devices, control devices like emergency stop buttons, and personal protective equipment; and
- *'software' measures* which rely on people, such as following safe systems of work, methods for selecting equipment, and information, instruction and training.[1]

We will now explore the most important hardware and software measures as they relate to work equipment safety.

2. Selecting the right equipment for the job

Risk can be avoided or significantly reduced through the choice of the right equipment. This applies to equipment in normal everyday use, as well as equipment used during non-routine operations such as cleaning and maintenance. When selecting any piece of work equipment it is important that it is right for the job it will be used for. There are a number of different factors that need to be considered before a piece of equipment is selected.

In what working conditions will the equipment be used?

EXAMPLE

If you intend to use an electrical tool in wet conditions, it is much safer to choose one which runs on batteries rather than one which runs on mains voltage.

What additional risks are there?

You need to also take into account any additional risks caused by the use of a particular piece of work equipment.

EXAMPLE

It may be safer in the wet to use compressed air tools. These, however, are likely to be noisier, particularly in confined spaces.

What about the worker?

You also need to think about the worker who is using the equipment, considering their size and ensuring they do not have to exert too much strain to use the equipment. The equipment should also be easy to operate for them.

EXAMPLE

Where appropriate, left-handed tools should be provided.

Is the equipment 'CE marked'?

In Europe a formal system exists which requires manufacturers and suppliers to ensure that machinery and some other equipment is safe when supplied. To show that this has been done they will then attach a 'CE mark'. Employers should always select machinery which has this mark. If equipment is imported into Europe from elsewhere which needs to be CE marked then it is the employer's duty to carry out a formal assessment to ensure it conforms to relevant standards. Buying a CE-marked item does not guarantee it is safe. It is only a claim from the manufacturer. The employer still needs to satisfy themselves that the item is safe before it is used.

3. The equipment is used safely and properly maintained

How many times have you used a screwdriver to open a tin of paint, damaging the head of the screwdriver in the process? Work equipment should only be used in conditions and for jobs for which it is suitable.

Examples of the types of hazards which might arise from the use of work equipment include:

- equipment coming apart or breaking and items being thrown out of the machine, possibly at high speed, e.g. an abrasive cutting-disc bursting on a hand-held angle grinder;
- material falling from equipment, e.g. someone working from a ladder and dropping tools and equipment on people below;
- material held in the equipment being unexpectedly thrown out, e.g. wood thrown out from a spindle-moulding machine;
- overheating or fire, and explosion of the equipment due to pressure build-up;
- explosion of substances in the equipment or during its operation, e.g. welding equipment being used on tanks containing petrol residues.

The general requirements for work equipment

Managers and supervisors need to ensure that workers use the equipment they provide safely. Here are some things that should be considered:

- Are controls easy to access and easily operated?
- Are emergency controls fitted and working correctly?

- Is the equipment being used in the right environment, e.g. is it safe for use in wet environments?
- Is the equipment stable so that it does not move when operated?
- Are the guards that are needed fitted and in use?
- Is a safe system of work in place, e.g. when working on a woodworking circular saw, are push-sticks or jigs being used to keep fingers away from the blade?

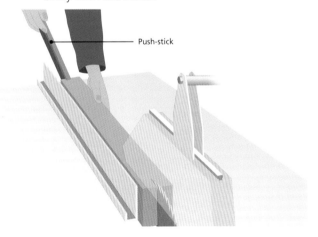

Using a push-stick with a table saw

- Is the workspace around the equipment clear and unobstructed?
- Is the correct PPE available and being used?
- Is there sufficient general and local lighting?
- Does the equipment have clear markings and have any necessary warnings been given?

The importance of clean equipment which has been adequately maintained cannot be stressed too highly. It is also important that any maintenance is conducted safely, whether by the operator or by maintenance staff. Well-maintained equipment is not only safer but is also more efficient and its performance will not deteriorate to the extent that it puts people at risk. The frequency at which maintenance needs to be carried out is dependent upon many things, such as how often the equipment is used and in what conditions, but this is normally something that the manufacturer will advise on.

Has the equipment been inspected?

It is good practice for operators of work equipment to carry out regular inspections to ensure that the equipment is still fit for purpose and that any damage or deterioration has been identified. In certain circumstances these inspections should be more formal, involve some degree of testing and should be carried out by a competent person. These are often called a 'thorough examination', which is supplemented by regular visual checks by the operator. Written records of these inspections should be kept.

EXAMPLE

1. When should a passenger lift be inspected by a competent person?
The position in the UK, according to legal and Health and Safety Executive requirements, is that passenger lifts are examined:

- before being put into service for the first time;
- after installation or reassembly on a new site (where safety depends on installation conditions);
- at least every six months or in accordance with an examination scheme; and
- if any 'exceptional circumstances' occur such as damage to, or failure of, the lift; long periods out of use; or a major change in operating conditions which is likely to affect the integrity of the equipment.[2]

2. What inspections/checks could the operator do between formal inspections?
User inspections would normally include visual and functional checks, that any alarms and safety interlocks operate correctly and lift doors cannot be opened from the landing side unless the lift is in place.

Work equipment should only be used by people who have received the proper information, instruction and training. This should be accompanied by suitable safety measures like protective devices, markings and warnings.

The UK Health and Safety Executive states that "information and written instructions you provide should cover:

(a) all health and safety aspects arising from the use of the work equipment;

(b) any limitations on these uses;

(c) any foreseeable difficulties that could arise;

(d) the methods to deal with them; and

(e) using any conclusions drawn from experience using the work equipment, you should either record them or take steps to ensure that all appropriate members of the workforce are aware of them."[3]

Workers need to be competent to use the work equipment provided. The level of training needed is likely to be greatest when someone starts the job. Training should also be refreshed at regular intervals and updated if the risks to which people are exposed change because new technology, work processes or machines are introduced. In low risk situations, this training can be done informally. For higher risk or more complex situations, training should be more formal and in-depth. In very high risk situations like operating chainsaws and fork-lift trucks, formal proof of competence is needed before the equipment can be used.

All workers should be competent to use work equipment regardless of their age. Training and proper supervision of young people is, however, particularly important because of their age and lack of experience with work.

Any workers who supervise or manage the use of work equipment must also receive adequate training for the purposes of health and safety. This should include training in the methods which may be adopted when using the work equipment, any risks which such use may entail and precautions to be taken to reduce the risk of injury during use.

Work equipment hazards and controls

We are now going to look at four examples of work equipment, identifying the most likely hazards that you would need to cover in a risk assessment, together with some likely control measures, although these will very much depend on particular circumstances.

1. The hazards and misuse of hand tools (e.g. knives)

HAZARDS	CONTROLS
Cutting/stabbing of self.	Redesign process to reduce need for trimming. Make sure knives are sharp and well maintained to avoid over-exertion. Use safe knives/cutters. Use of PPE like chain-mail gloves, particularly for butchers and pattern cutters. Make sure knives are safely stored, e.g. retracted when not in use. Safe use, e.g. cut away from hand/body. Knife handles which are comfortable and easy to grip. Availability of left- or right-handed tools. Regular inspection of the tools to look for defects.
Cutting/stabbing of others.	Enough space around to cut and proper lighting.

2. Portable power tools (e.g. portable drill)

HAZARDS	CONTROLS
Contact with rotating drill.	Safe use – specify a drill with sufficient power and correct drill bit for job to ensure that operator does not have to use undue force. Ensure bit is secure.
Entanglement around rotating drill.	No loose parts of clothing and tie back hair.
Noise and vibration.	PPE for noise and vibration (eye protection/gloves) although must ensure sufficient grip. Drill properly maintained. Select low vibration/noise tools.
Dust.	Use dust suppression techniques. (Other tools can have local dust extraction systems fitted.)
Electrocution.	Regular examination of tool. Alternative power sources, e.g. reduced voltage/battery powered.

HAZARDS	CONTROLS
Hands come into contact with blade.	Do not overfeed paper into the machine. Guard is fitted which prevents access to blade. Interlock device on bin prevents access to moving blade inside the machine when active.
Clothing or hair becomes entangled in blade.	Keep hair and clothing (e.g. a tie) away from the shredder opening when in operation. Hold to run device (machine will only work with button held) on operating switch.
Children contacting equipment in use.	If working from home, keep children away from shredder as their fingers may be smaller than guard.

4.   Equipment for working at height (i.e. ladders)

HAZARDS	CONTROLS
Falling from height.	Avoid work at height. Use correctly: for light work only and consider use of other access equipment such as tower scaffolds. Ladder in good condition and inspected regularly, including daily checks by user.
Being blown off ladder due to weather conditions, particularly when carrying long lengths of materials.	Avoid going up in high winds; avoid carrying things up and down (maintain 3 points of contact).
Contact with overhead cables.	Look out for any overhead cables and keep a safe distance away.
Ladder slipping.	Ladder positioned so that it won't slip (at angle of 75 degrees). Ladder secured to prevent movement. Should extend 1 metre above a landing place. Placed against a solid surface. Floor surface clean and level.
Dropping materials on passers-by.	Ensure clear warning signs displayed and people are not allowed to walk underneath. Secure tools so that they are not dropped. Safe method to bring materials to ground.
Obstruction.	Carefully place ladder and use barriers/warning signs.

To dispel a myth, the use of ladders has not been 'banned by health and safety'. Ladders can be and are safely used every day. However, work at height should be avoided if possible and ladders are only used:

- if more suitable work equipment is not justified due to the low level of risk and short duration of use; or
- if there are features on site which the employer can't alter.

Read the following account of an accident.

A window cleaner sustained a broken arm and ankle when he fell 2.5 m from a ladder while cleaning the windows of a two-storey office on an industrial estate. The ladder was at an acute angle in order to reach the top windows; was not secured or 'footed' by a second person; and the ground was slippery with moss. The ladder slipped while the window cleaner was reaching over to an area which he could not quite get the ladder to reach.

What might have helped to prevent this accident? (Consider the part played by both the window cleaner and the office company).

You might have included the following in your answer:

- *window cleaner* – use extendable poles; foot or secure the ladder; correct angle for the ladder; longer ladder to avoid over-reaching; refusing to clean inaccessible windows; in exceptional cases use access equipment, e.g. cherry picker;
- *office company* – clean up the moss so less slippery; consider alternative methods to clean inaccessible windows, e.g. fitting reversible windows which can be cleaned from the inside; ask for method statement from window cleaner.

Note: a "method statement" is a written statement describing the way the work will be done (usually step-by-step), the equipment to be used and safety precautions to be in place.

References

1   HSE INDG291 *Simple guide to the Provision and Use of Work Equipment Regulations 1998* (www.hse.gov.uk/pubns/indg291.pdf)
2   HSE INDG339(rev1) *Thorough examination and testing of lifts* (www.hse.gov.uk/pubns/indg339.pdf)
3   HSE ACoP L22 (3rd ed.) *Safe use of work equipment* (www.hse.gov.uk/pubns/priced/l22.pdf)

Practice Questions

Q13 It is a requirement that all users of work equipment are provided with training. Which should be covered in the training?
- A   Availability of welfare facilities
- B   How to carry out pre-use checks
- C   The manufacturing history of the supplier
- D   Where to obtain manufacturer's instructions

Q14 Which safety factor does an employer need to consider when selecting work equipment?
- A   The colour of the equipment
- B   The delivery time
- C   The environment the equipment will be used in
- D   The length of the guarantee period

Element 5 Transport safety

This element focuses on traffic and transport in and around the workplace, the hazards that vehicles present and ways to reduce the risk of injury to people.

On completion of this element, you should be able to:

5.1 Identify the hazards presented by the movement of vehicles in the workplace and the appropriate control measures

The movement of vehicles – hazards and controls

Following on from the previous element, this element refers to another aspect of work equipment. In this case it is called self-propelled work equipment or, more simply, vehicles used either at or for work such as tractors, dumper trucks, fork-lift trucks, ambulances, etc. All of the general safety requirements discussed in Element 4 will apply to this element and here we will only discuss those hazards and controls which are specific to vehicle safety. We will discuss issues associated with driving and operating vehicles for the operator as well as pedestrians, and associated hazards such as falling from height while sheeting a load.

Sheeting on a lorry load

We saw in Element 3 that vehicle-related accidents account for many work-related fatal accidents. The Health and safety Executive figures we looked at do not take into account vehicle accidents when on the public roads. If they did, as they do in many countries, the fatal accident figures would be much higher.

The main hazards that vehicle operators will encounter are:

Loss of control and overturning of vehicles
There are many factors which may make loss of control and overturning more likely. These include:

- wet and uneven ground;
- excessive or sudden gradients (slopes);
- excessive speeds;
- incorrect tyre pressures;
- sudden changes in direction; and
- inappropriately carried or secured loads and attachments.

Collisions with other vehicles, pedestrians and fixed objects
These can occur both off and on the public roads. People can be struck by the vehicle, run over or trapped against objects such as racking, walls and other fixed objects. Striking fixed objects such as racking can also dislodge loads and materials, causing them to fall onto the operator or pedestrians.

Associated hazards
These include:

- falling from height;
- contact with moving machinery, such as rotating drive-shafts;
- objects falling onto the operator from the vehicle because they are not correctly stowed; and
- the vehicle body itself trapping the operator, e.g. when undertaking maintenance or repair like changing tyres.

The UK Health and safety Executive refers to three types of transport safety controls[1] which we will explore in more detail:

- *Safe site*;
- *Safe driver*; and
- *Safe vehicle.*

Added to these is:

- *Safe operation.*

Safe site

- Make sure that all vehicle movements are properly risk-assessed and managed. Drawing a site plan or sketch will be helpful showing parking, location of reception or other key areas, route to take through the site, and location of (un)loading areas. Traffic routes should be well-planned (e.g. one-way systems, speed limits, etc.) and proper safety signage displayed. Reversing should be avoided wherever possible. Extra care should be taken at vehicle crossing points. Ensure visitors to the site are aware of the site rules.

- If there are areas where vehicles drop off, load/unload or reverse then these should be signed and specific rules may be needed, e.g. use of banksmen (persons to direct the movement of vehicles and suspended loads on cranes).

Banksman directing unloading

- The employer will need to consider environmental factors (e.g. visibility, gradients, changes of level, surface conditions, and adequate lighting).

- Means of segregating pedestrians and vehicles may be needed. These may include protective measures for people and structures (e.g. barriers, kerbs, etc.) or where these are not possible, floor markings, road traffic signs, mirrors, and warnings of vehicle approach and reversing (such as reversing beepers and flashing beacons).

Safe driver

- The need for competent vehicle operators cannot be overstressed. Just because someone can drive a car does not mean that they can operate other vehicles such as mini-buses or excavators without the necessary training. In the UK and many other countries, formal systems for the certification of operators of certain vehicles (e.g. fork-lift trucks) exist.

- It is important that this training and competence assessment is repeated at regular intervals. Managers must ensure that vehicle operators are performing vehicle operations safely and correctly and that they are obeying site rules such as speed limits.

- The fitness of the worker to operate a vehicle should be assessed. Some health conditions such as back and neck disorders, epilepsy, etc. may mean that operators are not fit to operate some vehicles.

The movement of vehicles – hazards and controls

Safe vehicle

- The most important thing is to first choose the right vehicle for the job.

EXAMPLE

It is not advisable to use a normal counterbalance fork-lift truck on rough terrain, as it is likely to overturn. In this case a rough-terrain fork-lift should be used.

- Vehicles must be well-maintained; in particular the tyres, brakes and mirrors. Employers can implement a system of user checks which include both start-up and daily checks. These checks cover basics such as tyres, horn, etc. This system must also include a clear procedure for reporting faults on the vehicle. Vehicle maintenance can in itself provide risks.

EXAMPLE

Tipping vehicle bodies or tilting cabs should always be propped when people work under them.

- Some vehicles are at risk of rolling over, with the potential consequence of crushing the operator and any passengers. If this can occur, the vehicle should be fitted with a system for minimising this risk. This can consist of counterbalance weights or protective structures often known as roll-over protective structures or "ROPS". Restraint systems, most commonly seat belts, should also be worn by people riding on or being carried by vehicles if there is a risk of falling out and/or being crushed by the vehicle in the event of it rolling over.

Roll-over protective structure

- Another common risk is that of injury from objects falling on operators and passengers while the work equipment is in use.

EXAMPLE

Objects may fall on a fork-lift truck operator when moving a load from the top of some racking to the floor. If this is a significant risk then a falling object protection system (FOP) should be provided.

- If people have to climb on vehicles then stop them from falling by providing ladders, guardrails, handholds and walkways. As a last resort consider harnesses. Better still, develop a system such that they don't need to climb on the vehicle at all, e.g. operating controls or checking gauges from the ground. Use automated or mechanical systems for the sheeting of vehicles, or manual sheeting systems which don't require people to go up on the vehicle.

- Some vehicles are designed and operated in a way which makes it difficult for the operator to see all round, e.g. refuse collection vehicles. This is particularly important when reversing and turning. In this case systems such as the use of banksmen; warning systems for vehicle manoeuvring like flashing beacons, reversing alarms, etc.; and devices which increase the field of vision (plane, angled and curved mirrors; Fresnel (blind spot) lenses and in some cases CCTV) are useful.

Safe operation

Here we are referring to things like loading/unloading, stacking, lifting, and travelling with a load.

- The operation of the vehicle can pose significant risks even after considering all of the issues we've mentioned. In this case a safe system of work should be developed for the operation of the vehicle. As an example we will look at one of the most dangerous of the common pieces of mobile work equipment, fork-lift trucks. Fork-lift truck operation can be particularly hazardous. One serious hazard is that the truck is liable to overturn. This can be a particular issue if the truck is used with the load on raised forks. This raises the centre of gravity of the truck/load combination so that if the truck changes direction rapidly or moves across a slope, particularly sideways along the slope, it can easily tip over.

EXAMPLE

Safe system of work for a fork-lift truck:

- Only use trained drivers familiar with the fork-lift truck, the terrain and the tasks carried out.
- Ensure the fork-lift truck and attachments are suitable for the work and the terrain.
- Position the forks and any attachments correctly.
- Avoid uneven and unstable ground.
- Put the handbrake on while lifting or lowering loads.
- Do not drive forwards if the driver cannot see over the load.
- Reverse down gradients with a load on the forks.
- Drive carefully and slowly on wet ground and across gradients.
- Do not park or leave fork-lift trucks on gradients.
- Do not leave the keys in the fork-lift truck when unattended.
- Ensure statutory inspections and examinations, and regular maintenance are carried out.

Consider how transport safety could be improved in your workplace. Suggest three ways.

Alternatively, if your company has few traffic movements, consider the car park or the traffic system at a site you are familiar with such as a supermarket or college. As above suggest three ways in which it could be improved.

Ways to improve transport safety could include:

- A one-way traffic-flow system around the works.
- An appropriate speed limit for vehicle movements.
- Designated specific areas off-road where vehicles load and unload.
- Designated separate parking areas for works vehicles and private cars.
- Separation of pedestrians from vehicles by the use of barriers, kerbs, etc.
- Use of road signs, markings, and warnings such as flashing beacons to alert users to the dangers.
- Pedestrian crossings with markings and lights for night operation.
- Have separate entrances and exits for vehicles and people.
- The provision of adequate lighting.
- Ensure that pedestrians in areas where vehicles are in use wear high-visibility garments.
- A proper maintenance programme for all works vehicles.
- Proper training for all works drivers.

References

1   HSE INDG199(rev1)
    Workplace transport safety – An overview
    (www.hse.gov.uk/pubns/indg199.pdf)

Practice Questions

Q15 Which is NOT a control measure to reduce the risk to pedestrians from vehicles on site?

   A   Audible and visual warnings on all vehicles
   B   Barriers
   C   The provision of safety boots to all workers
   D   The provision of worker training on road safety

Q16 Which may cause a fork-lift truck to overturn?

   A   Driving too slowly
   B   Driving with the load in a raised position
   C   Driving on a flat surface
   D   The rear indicator lights not working

Hazards and controls associated with working with electricity

This element focuses on electrical safety. Electricity is the most common form of power and its use to power machinery, and heat and light our homes is almost universal across the world. Unfortunately, electricity can kill and injure people. *You should note that any work on electrical equipment and systems is not for the non-expert and should always be done by a competent person.*

Learning outcomes

On completion of this element, you should be able to:

6.1 Identify the hazards associated with the use of electricity in the workplace

6.2 Identify the control measures that need to be taken when working with electrical systems or using electrical equipment

Hazards associated with the use of electricity in the workplace

In the UK about 1,000 electrical accidents at work are reported to the Health and Safety Executive each year and about 25 people die of their injuries. In order to understand why electricity is dangerous, you first need to know a little about what it is and how it works.

1. What is electricity?

All materials contain electrically charged particles called electrons. In some materials, the electrons can be made to flow through the material to produce an *electric current*. Current is measured in units called amperes, often shortened to amps (symbol A). Smaller currents are measured in milliamps (mA).

To produce current, the electrons are moved by electro-motive force around a *circuit*, which is measured by a potential difference, called the *voltage*. For a given voltage, the size of the current is determined by a property of the circuit called the *resistance*. Some materials have little resistance and allow electricity to pass through them easily. These are called *conductors*. Good conductors are metals like copper. Some materials do not allow current to pass through them easily, and are called *insulators*. Water can have the effect of reducing resistance and therefore when used in the wet some equipment can be more dangerous than when used in dry conditions.

When a circuit has a current flowing through it, it is referred to as being "*live*" (or "*hot*"); when the current is switched off or isolated from the circuit, it is called "*dead*".

Friction can generate an electric charge between two objects which are not good conductors. This is called *static electricity*. This can often be felt as a shock when it discharges to earth. Static can be heard as the crackle when combing your hair. Static charges are unlikely to be enough to hurt you, but they can easily be enough to ignite flammable vapours.

To help you understand these principles better, we can use the illustration of water running through a pipe by gravity.

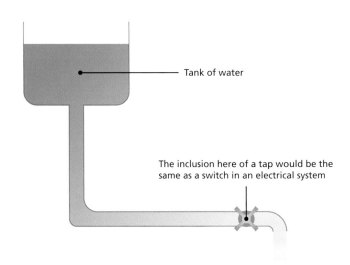

Tank of water

The inclusion here of a tap would be the same as a switch in an electrical system

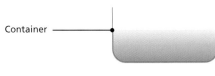

Container

Water system

The water flowing through the pipe represents the current. The tank of water with a 'head of water' represents the potential difference (or voltage). The force that will drive the water along the pipe is gravity. But for gravity to work, the tank of water has to be higher than the container receiving the water. This is the same as the potential difference or voltage.

The rougher or narrower the inside of the pipe the slower the rate of flow will be. This is similar to the effect of the resistance. A conductor with a high resistance cuts down the flow of electric charge.

The Health and Safety Executive states that in the UK most deaths and injuries resulting from contact with an electrical charge arise from:

- use of badly maintained electrical equipment, in particular portable appliances;
- activities near overhead power lines, like contacting the lines with long items of work equipment such as ladders or lengths of material, fishing rods, etc.;
- contact with underground power cables, often during excavation work;
- work on or with mains electricity supplies (230 volts in the UK);
- use of unsuitable electrical equipment in wet or explosive areas.

They also state that the risks of injury from electricity are greatest in harsh conditions, particularly in wet surroundings, outdoors and in cramped spaces with a lot of metalwork, such as when working inside a tank.[1]

3. Hazards of electricity

The main hazards and risks are:

Electric shock from contact with electricity

When the body comes into contact with a live source of electrical energy, a current will flow through the body from the point of contact (e.g. a hand) to a point in contact with the ground (an earth) such as a foot. This causes a convulsion of the body which is called an electric shock. Electric shock can cause pain, burns at the points of entry and exit (and internally as the current flows through the body), and muscle contractions or convulsions. These convulsions may tighten chest muscles, making breathing difficult, and stop the heart beating. An electrical current of around 10mA will cause muscle contraction. In such a situation, it may not be possible to let go of the live electrical source. The severity of the shock will depend on:

- the size of the current passing through the body;
- the duration of the electric current; and
- the path of the electric current through the body (paths which pass through the heart are particularly dangerous).

Contact with mains voltage, which produces a current of 60mA and above, can easily be fatal, particularly if the conditions are wet, which lowers the body's total resistance. In these cases the normal rhythm of the heart can be affected (ventricular fibrillation) or stop altogether (cardiac arrest).

Electrical burns

These are due to the heating effect caused by the passage of electric current through body tissues. They can be very severe as they tend to penetrate deep into the body's tissues. They are usually painful and can be very slow to heal with resultant scarring.

Contact with the electricity can be directly from the source or indirectly from some other conducting material. Equipment may be wrongly connected or damaged so that the outside metal parts become live, or metal or other conducting materials around the source become live.

Fires and explosions resulting from electricity

Electrical equipment that is damaged, overloaded (items needing or using more current than the circuit can withstand), and poorly maintained can get very hot, which can in turn lead to fires and explosions. Likewise, a short-circuit (an unintended flow of current between two conductors) also causes sparks and can start fires and explosions. Very low voltage electrical sparks can have enough energy to ignite flammable substances such as in a paint spray booth.

Secondary hazards and risks

These may arise after an individual receives an electric shock.

> **EXAMPLE**
> Physical injury from falling, particularly from a height.

Hazards associated with the use of electricity in the workplace

Risks specifically associated with portable electrical equipment

The term "portable electrical equipment" refers to devices that have a cable and plug and which are portable or can easily be moved from place to place. It includes kettles, heaters, portable drills, radios, etc. It is estimated that nearly a quarter of all reportable electrical accidents involve portable equipment. Because such equipment is moved on a regular basis, it can easily become damaged, particularly the cable and the plug. It may also be subjected to, and more vulnerable to, wear or harsh treatment. This damage can result in live electrical conductors being exposed, and electrical fires.[2]

Risks from charged storage equipment (batteries, capacitors, etc.)

Some devices are designed to store energy for use at a later time. Batteries do this by converting chemical energy into electric energy. Some batteries are designed to be re-charged, while others are not. The UK Health and Safety Executive estimates that every year at least 25 people are seriously injured when using batteries at work. Hazards and risks include:

- explosion after short-circuiting of the battery terminals;
- electrocution and burns from high-voltage battery packs;
- exposure to the hazardous chemicals contained in batteries;
- hydrogen and oxygen are usually produced inside a battery when it is being charged, and these gases can cause an explosion.[3]

Common injuries include electric shocks; burns to the face, eyes and hands; wounds from flying pieces of metal and plastic; and burns from metal objects that have become very hot.

The UK Health and Safety Executive, in its publication INDG139 *Using electric storage batteries safely*, advises that the following precautions should be taken:

- Wear gloves and suitable eye protection, preferably goggles or a visor.
- Wear a protective apron and suitable boots when handling battery chemicals.
- Ensure no metal objects can fall onto the battery or bridge across its terminals.
- Keep sources of ignition, such as flames, sparks, electrical equipment, hot objects and mobile phones well away from batteries that are being or have been recently charged, or are being moved.
- Use suitable, single-ended tools with insulated handles.
- Fit temporary plastic covers over the battery terminals.
- Charge batteries in a dedicated, well-ventilated area.
- Share the load with a workmate when lifting heavy batteries.
- Use insulated lifting equipment and check there are no tripping hazards.
- Wash hands thoroughly after working with batteries.

Control measures associated with working with electricity

There are some things which seem like common sense which we often forget to do. These can present unnecessary risk. For example, tools and power socket-outlets should be switched off before plugging in or unplugging. It is also important to emphasise that work involving electricity should be undertaken by a trained and competent person.

The important thing to remember when working with electrical systems is that you should *never* work on or near exposed live parts unless it is absolutely necessary (usually only for testing). So, before work commences, switch off the system and isolate it (make sure it can't be switched on again) by removing the fuses, locking the isolator switch with a padlock, and placing a warning notice on the system.

If it is necessary to work on live systems, then very strict health and safety systems should be followed to protect both the workers and anyone else who may be in the area, but this is outside the scope of this course book. If any equipment is decommissioned, it should be disconnected from all sources of electrical supply and isolated. Never assume this has been done if you start to work on equipment that you think is disconnected.

1. Selection and suitability of equipment

The first issues that should be considered are the *design*, *construction* and *installation* of new electrical systems and equipment, which should be to a suitable standard. This should cover all foreseeable uses as well as maintenance, cleaning and repair. Detailed safety standards are produced by such organisations as the Institution of Electrical Engineers in the UK and should be followed at all times.

You must also be sure that the equipment is suitable for the environment in which it is being used, for example:

* suitable for wet conditions;
* resistant to mechanical damage, etc.

Electrical risks can sometimes be eliminated by using air-, hydraulic-, hand- or cartridge-powered equipment.

It is also important that machinery can be switched off quickly. There should be an easily accessible and clearly identified switch near each fixed machine to cut off power in an emergency. This is equally true for portable equipment, where it is best to use socket-outlets which are close to where you are working, so that equipment can be easily disconnected if necessary.

Other points that the Health and Safety Executive advise[1] are:

* The outer sheath of the ends of flexible cables should always be firmly clamped, to stop the wires (particularly the earth) pulling out of the terminals.
* Use proper connectors or cable couplers to join lengths of cable.
* Do not use plastic strips of connector blocks covered in insulating tape.

2. Protective measures

There are a number of common protective devices and systems which are used to help protect one or more of the electrical system, the equipment and the worker.

Fuses
These are used to prevent an over-current (a current surge larger than the intended supply) within a system. A fuse is designed to intentionally break the electrical circuit by 'burning out' or breaking when an excessive current passes through it. Fuses are not generally considered a protective device for people's safety, because they act too slowly. They provide protection for electrical equipment. It is important that a correctly rated fuse is used, to ensure that it will burn out at a current which is lower than that which could damage the equipment.

EXAMPLE
An item (e.g. a radio) needing only 4 amps will be protected by a 5A fuse, which will burn out at a current higher than 5 amps and protect the radio.

Earthing
Electricity will always seek to travel to earth along the path of least resistance. Earthing provides a path for electricity to move safely from any damaged or broken fixture or appliance back to earth. Lack of good earth connections is said to be the commonest electrical safety problem. Remember that any conductive parts of equipment which aren't live could become so in a fault condition. Any item of equipment which is mains-powered should be correctly fitted with a protective (safety) earth or be double-

Control measures associated with working with electricity

insulated (see later). The earthing should be strong enough to safely discharge the electrical energy to earth.

Isolation

As we saw earlier, *isolation* means we physically separate an item of electrical equipment or an electrical circuit from the source of electric power. We do this by first switching it off, then locking the isolator ("lock-off") switch with a padlock (sometimes fuses may need to be removed) and placing safety warning notices on the switch. Where more than one electrician needs to work on the same system, a hasp that each electrician can place their own padlock into should be used. The circuit cannot be switched on again until all padlocks are removed.

Reduced low voltage systems

One of the best ways of reducing the risk of injury from the use of electrical equipment is to limit the supply voltage to the lowest possible level needed to operate the equipment. The voltage should be low enough so that any resultant current, which in a fault condition could injure the worker, is lower than that which could cause serious injury.

EXAMPLE

110V portable tools (centre-tapped-to-earth) are commonly used on many construction sites. These can still be dangerous though, particularly in wet conditions. It is better in these cases to use battery-operated tools.

Wherever possible, temporary lighting systems should be supplied at very low voltages of 25V or less.

Residual current devices

A residual current device (RCD) acts as a safety trip device when there is a fault. RCDs detect very small leakages of electric current to earth and quickly cut off the electricity supply. They are normally rated as 30mA/30ms (i.e. the device will operate when it detects a leakage current of 30mA) devices. The mistake that many people make is to ignore an RCD when it trips, forgetting that this is a sign that there is a fault. The system should be checked before it is used again. Also, if the RCD is fitted with a test button, this should be used regularly to check that the RCD's mechanism is working properly.[4]

Double insulation

Insulation provides protection between the worker and live conductors. Most often this is sheathing around the conductors. Equipment which is not earthed is usually 'double-insulated' or 'Class II' and in Europe is marked with the 'double square' symbol. The live conductors in double-insulated equipment are covered by two separate layers of insulation, thereby doubling the potential protection from the danger arising from insulation failure. This avoids the need for separate earthing and is most often used for portable equipment.

Double insulation symbol

3. Inspection and maintenance strategies

Regular inspection, testing and maintenance of electrical systems, equipment, sockets and cables must also be carried out at suitable intervals if danger would otherwise result. Suspect or faulty equipment is taken out of use and labelled as such. It is important that damaged equipment, sockets or sections of cable are replaced completely as soon as possible.

The UK Health and Safety Executive recommends that maintenance, particularly of portable equipment, should consist of:

- checks by the user;
- formal visual inspections by a person trained and appointed to carry them out;
- combined inspection and tests by an electrically competent person.

User checks

Users of electrical equipment should check themselves that the item is safe to use before use. No attempt should be made to open or remove covers, etc. from the item. Instead, just check that:

- the plug is intact and not damaged;
- there are no burn marks around the pins on the plug, and that they are not bent;
- the cable is clamped into the plug – no inner cables or bare wires are exposed;
- the cable itself is intact – there are no cracks or splits, abrasion damage or burn marks;

- the body of the item of equipment is not damaged, burned, cracked, etc.; and
- the cable into the equipment is clamped and secure, with no inner cables or bare wires showing.[2]

Formal inspection and tests

At regular intervals, *formal visual inspections* should be carried out by a trained and competent person. These will include all of the items checked by the user, but will also include taking the plug apart to check security of connections, cable clamp, etc. and the condition and security of the fuse. At these inspections it is also appropriate to take off covers and look at the connections and for other signs of deterioration and damage inside the item of equipment.

Combined inspection and tests will be required where "there is reason to suppose the equipment may be defective (but this cannot be confirmed by visual inspection)".[5] These checks (sometimes referred to as Portable Appliance Tests – or PAT) are useful as some faults, such as a broken earth wire within a flexible cable, or deterioration of insulation integrity, cannot be detected by visual inspection alone. The Health and Safety Executive recommends that this type of check should be carried out "after any repair, modification or similar work" and "at periods appropriate to the equipment, the manner and frequency of use and the environment".[5] Again, this testing must be done by trained, competent persons.

What points would you look for in a visual inspection of a portable electrical appliance? You can include both user checks and formal visual inspections here, but remember that inspections should always be undertaken by a competent person and this exercise is only for educational purposes.

Based on Health and Safety Executive Guidance at www.hse.gov.uk/electricity/electricequip.htm#condition and in INDG236[2]:

- Begin by switching off and unplugging the equipment.
- Check that the plug is correctly wired (but only if you are competent to do so and unless a moulded plug is fitted), is not damaged and that the cable is properly secured with no internal wires visible.
- Check that the pins in the plug are not burned or bent.
- Ensure that the fuse is correctly rated by checking the equipment rating plate (a label on the item showing the technical specifications) or instruction book.
- Check that the electrical cable is not damaged and has not been repaired with insulating tape or an unsuitable connector.
- Check that the outer sheath of the cable is effectively secured where it enters the plug or the equipment. Obvious evidence to the contrary would be if the coloured insulation of the internal cable cores were showing.
- Check that the outer cover or casing of the equipment is not damaged.
- Check that the cable terminations are secure and correct, including an earth where appropriate.
- Check for burn marks or staining that would suggest that the equipment is overheating.
- Position any trailing wires so that they are not a trip hazard and are less likely to get damaged.

Frequency of inspection, testing and maintenance

This will depend on:

- the type of equipment;
- how often it is used;
- what it is used for; and
- the environment in which it operates.

Generally, portable appliances present the greatest danger. In the UK, the Institution of Electrical Engineers provides guidance on this. The Health and Safety Executive document HSG107 *Maintaining portable and transportable electrical equipment* also gives advice on formal inspection and tests.

Records of inspection and testing

These should be kept, as they may be useful in keeping a log of all equipment and looking for areas where higher than average faults or damage are occurring.

Underground power cables

If carrying out any excavation work, always assume that underground service cables such as electric, gas, etc. cables will be present unless it is certain that they are not. Up-to-date service plans should be consulted, although this is not always reliable as the position of cables can be wrongly included. If in any doubt, use a cable avoidance tool and implement safe digging practice (e.g. avoid use of heavy excavators and power drills – only dig carefully by hand near cables and wear appropriate PPE, such as rubber safety footwear and insulated gloves). Accurate service plans can be obtained from organisations like the electricity companies and local authorities.[1,6]

Overhead power lines

Care should be taken when working or carrying material near to or underneath overhead power lines. Whatever voltage they carry (230V or 400KV), they are extremely dangerous. The UK Health and Safety Executive estimates that half of the fatal electrical accidents each year are caused by contact with overhead lines. These are dangerous not just because of the voltage, but also because the wires (conductors) are generally bare (uninsulated). Touching them, or in some cases even coming close to them with anything conductive (like the arm of a mechanical excavator) will result in flow of electricity down the conductive object, potentially resulting in an electric shock to any surrounding workers. This can also occur with wet or damp insulators like wood and plastic.

If working near live cables is unavoidable, it may be possible to have them switched off or the power diverted. If this cannot be done, you need to consider controls such as:

- Keeping a safe working distance from the cables and erecting ground-level barriers parallel to the overhead line.
- If you have to travel under the lines, restrict the width of any passageway under the wires and have rigid 'goal posts' erected at each end to act as gateways in the barriers running parallel to the overhead line. Be very aware of the height of any load and ensure that it cannot touch the lines. The safe clearance required beneath the overhead lines should be determined.
- Any plant, equipment or tools that could reach beyond the safe clearance limit should not be taken under the line. If working underneath, plant such as cranes and excavators should be modified by the addition of suitable physical restraints so that they cannot reach beyond the safe clearance limit.[7]

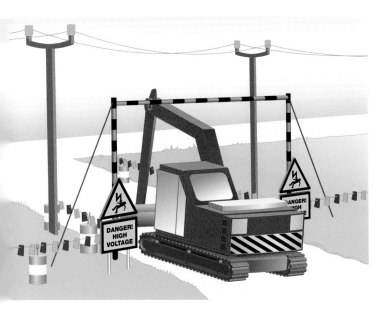

'Goal posts' to control height of vehicles moving beneath power lines

References/Practice Questions

References

1   HSE INDG231 *Electrical safety and you*
    (www.hse.gov.uk/pubns/indg231.pdf)

2   HSE INDG236 *Maintaining portable
    electrical equipment in offices and other
    low risk environments*
    (www.hse.gov.uk/pubns/indg236.pdf)

3   HSE INDG139(rev1)
    Using electric storage batteries safely
    (www.hse.gov.uk/pubns/indg139.pdf)

4   HSE INDG247 *Electrical safety for entertainers*
    (www.hse.gov.uk/pubns/indg247.pdf)

5   HSE HSG107 (2nd ed.) *Maintaining portable and
    transportable electrical equipment*
    (www.hse.gov.uk/pubns/priced/hsg107.pdf)

6   HSE HSG47 *Avoiding danger from
    underground services*
    (www.hse.gov.uk/pubns/priced/hsg47.pdf)

7   HSE GS6 (3rd ed.) *Avoidance of danger from
    overhead electric power lines*
    (www.hse.gov.uk/pubns/priced/gs6.pdf)

Practice Questions

Q17 Which is a risk associated with electricity?
    A   Corrosion
    B   Entrapment
    C   Fire
    D   Hearing loss

Q18 Which is a common cause of electric shock in
    the workplace?
    A   Wearing safety goggles
    B   Confined space working
    C   Not wearing head protection
    D   A non-qualified person working on an
        electric circuit

Q19 Which is correct?
    A   A residual current device (RCD) is easy to defeat
    B   A fuse will always protect someone from
        electric shock
    C   One of the most effective ways to reduce the risks
        from electricity is to use low voltage equipment
    D   Providing safety goggles and head protection will
        reduce the risk of electric shock to workers

Q20 Which is a suitable control measure to reduce
    the risk of electric shock?
    A   Health surveillance
    B   The provision of safety goggles
    C   The provision of a safety data sheet
    D   The use of low voltage tools

Element 7 Fire safety

This element focuses on fire safety as it applies to low- to medium-risk working environments. This will give you an overview of some of the general principles of fire safety. We will discuss the causes of fire, fire spread, some common control measures and the principles of fire risk assessment. This will **not** make you a competent fire risk assessor.

These general principles will also apply to high risk premises such as those having sleeping accommodation or storing large quantities of flammable chemicals, but the requirements of these organisations will be much more detailed. These types of premises are regulated much more closely and will normally have to produce very detailed risk assessments, control measures and emergency plans and are outside the scope of this course book.

Learning outcomes

On completion of this element, you should be able to:

7.1 Outline the common fire hazards in the workplace
7.2 Identify the benefits of adequate fire risk assessment and the matters which should be addressed when undertaking a basic fire risk assessment
7.3 Outline the basic principles of fire prevention and fire controls in the workplace

The common fire hazards in the workplace

1. What is fire?

Fire is the rapid process of combustion (or more technically oxidation) of a material causing heat, light and other products of combustion to be released.

2. The causes of fire

For a fire to start, three conditions must exist at the same time. There must be:

- fuel that will burn;
- an ignition source to initiate and sometimes sustain the fire until it can sustain itself by the further release of heat energy; and
- the presence of a source of oxygen.

This is often depicted as the 'fire triangle'.

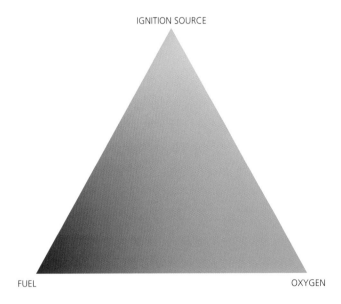

IGNITION SOURCE

FUEL

OXYGEN

Taking away one of these elements of the fire triangle will mean that the fire will be prevented or will be stopped (extinguished).

Sources of ignition

There are many sources of ignition which exist in typical workplaces, for example:

- naked flames from heaters, smoking, etc.;
- static electricity;
- welding and cutting tools;
- sparks from metal-grinding;
- sparks from electrical equipment (both from faults and from normal operation); and
- hot surfaces from heaters, poorly maintained equipment, etc.

Sources of fuel

There are likely to be many sources of fuel within most workplaces. Commonly these will include wood, plastics, foam, furniture and paper. There may also be:

- flammable liquids such as petrol and some solvents;
- dusts from wood, coal, grain and foodstuffs; and
- gases like hydrogen, which may be generated as part of a work process such as battery charging.

Sources of oxygen

The most common source of oxygen is the air around us. Only in very special circumstances will it be possible to exclude air from the working environment (e.g. the use of inert gases in computer suites). Oxygen may be stored as a gas, e.g. in cylinders, or certain chemicals, called oxidising substances, provide a source of oxygen when they are heated or react with other chemicals. These are not necessarily combustible, but they add or generate oxygen. Common examples are oxidising agents such as hydrogen peroxide and sodium hypochlorite (bleach).

Carry out a visual inspection of your workplace for possible sources of ignition, fuel and oxygen. How many can you identify?

If you have access to the Internet, you can find examples of what to look for in UK Communities and Local Government guidance, e.g. *Fire Safety Risk Assessment – Factories and Warehouses* (www.communities.gov.uk/documents/fire/pdf/145025.pdf), pages 14 to 16.

3. Fire classification

The types of fire are normally classified by their fuel source.[1]

CLASS OF FIRE	CHARACTERISTICS	HOW IT IS EXTINGUISHED			
A	Fires involving ordinary organic, solid combustibles such as wood, paper	WATER	WET CHEMICAL	FOAM SPRAY	ABC POWDER
B	Fires involving flammable liquids and liquefiable solids such as petrol	CARBON DIOXIDE		FOAM SPRAY	ABC POWDER
C	Fires involving flammable gases such as methane, propane	Gas fires should not be extinguished; this may leave unburned gases as an explosion risk.		Turn off the gas supply.	
D	Fires involving metals such as magnesium, aluminium, etc.	Special extinguishing media are required depending upon the metal involved.			
F	Fires involving cooking fat and oil in large catering establishments		WET CHEMICAL		

KEY

Water extinguisher

Wet chemical extinguisher

Foam spray extinguisher

Dry powder extinguisher

Carbon dioxide extinguisher

Fire extinguishers in Europe are mainly coloured red and have a band or circle of a second colour covering between 5% and 10% of the surface area of the extinguisher to indicate the contents. The circle or band colours are:

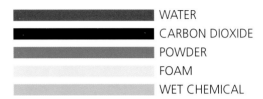

- WATER
- CARBON DIOXIDE
- POWDER
- FOAM
- WET CHEMICAL

4. Fire spread

Both the heat and the dangerous combustion products contained in smoke from fire can spread in a number of ways. These can be summarised as by convection; by conduction; and by radiation. The direct burning of objects can also spread heat and fire.

Convection

When air becomes warm, it becomes less dense and begins to rise. Colder, more dense air will in turn be drawn down to the fire, bringing a fresh source of oxygen. The rising warmer air with any accompanying burning debris will be spread to other parts of the building.

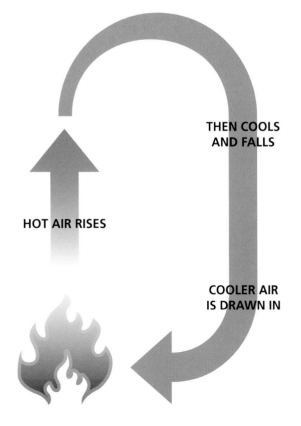

THEN COOLS AND FALLS

HOT AIR RISES

COOLER AIR IS DRAWN IN

Convection Currents

Conduction

Heat will transfer between neighbouring molecules of a substance. This transfer always takes place from a region of higher temperature to a region of lower temperature and occurs in solids. Liquids and gases are very poor conductors of heat. The process is called thermal conduction (to distinguish it from electrical conduction) but it is often referred to as simply conduction. Conduction occurs most rapidly and easily through a conducting material. Any combustible material which surrounds such a conductor will in turn become hot and could burn. Metals are excellent conductors of heat, and can present particular problems when used in the construction of structures, e.g. metal-frame buildings. Some materials which are poor conductors and cannot burn, e.g. concrete, are used to protect against fire. Probably the best known of these is asbestos, which unfortunately can be extremely hazardous to health due to its fibrous nature and its use is now banned.

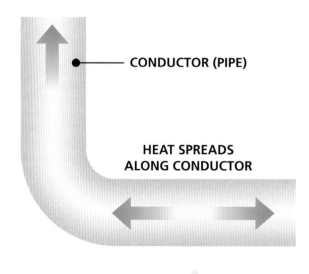

CONDUCTOR (PIPE)

HEAT SPREADS ALONG CONDUCTOR

Conduction

Radiation

Radiation is the transfer of heat from an object to its surroundings in the form of electromagnetic waves. Unlike convection and conduction no 'medium' (solid, liquid or gas) is needed. The best example of this is feeling the heat from the sun. All objects emit radiation but only when they are at a sufficiently high temperature does the process become significant. A piece of metal which is glowing red or white hot will be emitting radiant heat energy.

Direct burning

This is simply the action of materials catching fire from direct contact with other burning materials.

Fires in buildings and outdoors

Fires in buildings behave differently from those outdoors:

- The structure of buildings can both trap, and in some cases encourage, fire. Smoke and heat rising from the fire can get trapped by the roof and ceilings and then spread to form a deep layer over the entire room. As this happens, the smoke will pass through any holes or gaps in the structure such as ceiling voids and spread round the whole building.

- Outdoor fires can be intensified and spread quickly by such factors as dry vegetation, the presence of other combustibles and strong winds. Outdoor fires exhibit strong seasonal patterns, mainly due to the effect of the weather.

5. The common causes and consequences of fires in workplaces

In this subsection we will spend a little time looking at the official report figures for the UK. The situation may vary in other parts of the world.

If you are studying in the UK, how do these figures relate to your workplace?

If you are studying elsewhere in the world, try to find out the figures for your own country and relate them to your workplace.

Main causes of fire

The majority of fires occurring in non-domestic premises in the UK[2] affect:

- private garages and sheds (22%);
- retail distribution (14%);
- restaurants, cafes, public houses, etc. (9%);
- industrial premises (other than construction sites) (8%);
- recreational and other cultural services (6%).

The UK Communities and Local Government Department published a report in March 2010 which examined the causes of fires in commercial premises (*Examination of large loss fires in commercial buildings: Initial report*)[3]. It found the most likely cause (around 40%) to be *arson* – the deliberate ignition of fires, often multi-seated (i.e. more than one point where the fire started), often involving petrol or other flammable liquids, and often occurring at night.

The statistics show that certain buildings are more prone to arson than others, in particular private garages and sheds (65% deliberate); construction industry premises (57%); recreational and other cultural services premises (44%); and schools (44%).[2]

The main cause of *accidental* fires in non-domestic buildings in 2007 was found to be faulty electrical appliances and leads. These represented 32% of all fires. Faults which can result in fire include:

- overloading sockets by connecting too many appliances;

The common fire hazards in the workplace

- faulty or loose wiring which can lead to sparks; and
- damage or degradation of insulation around wires which can cause a short-circuit and lead to overheating.

The next most likely cause was misuse of equipment or appliances.

Other common causes of accidental fire in buildings were from smokers' materials; cooking oil fires; and horseplay ('playing with fire').

Other possible causes include:

- cooking appliances;
- heating appliances;
- blowlamps, welding and cutting equipment;
- sparks from grinders;
- electrical distribution; and
- candles.

Fire consequences

The main consequences from fire are death and serious injury. In 2007 there were 31,000 fires recorded in buildings other than dwellings. These resulted in 36 people dying, equivalent to about 1 death per 1,000 fires. There were 1,300 injuries or about 41 per 1,000 fires. Of these, 61% were accidental compared to over 80% of those in dwellings.[2]

Premises where fires have been shown to cause large numbers of serious injuries are elderly persons' homes; public administration premises, which includes police stations and prisons; and hostels/guest-houses/hotels.

There is fortunately a general downward trend since about 1995.

Almost half of all deaths relating to fire are caused by smoke or gas inhalation, with the remainder being from burns; a combination of effects from burns and smoke and other causes such as oxygen depletion; and injury from structural collapse.

Other consequences could include:

- structural damage to buildings;
- equipment and stock damage;
- delay and loss of business;
- damage from fire-fighting water/foam; and
- environmental damage, e.g. damage to wildlife.

Fire risk assessment

It is important that a *'responsible person'* takes management responsibility for fire safety. This person should have control over the premises and could be the owner or manager.

1. The role and benefits of adequate fire risk assessment

The 'responsible person' mentioned above should arrange for a risk assessment to be conducted by a competent person and make sure that any actions which are identified are carried out. They should also maintain a fire management plan.

UK Communities and Local Government (CLG) guidance on Fire Safety Risk Assessment[4] says that fire risk assessment provides an "organised and methodical look at your premises, the activities carried on there and the likelihood that a fire could start and cause harm to those in and around the premises". It goes on to say that "The aims of the fire risk assessment are:

- to identify the fire hazards.
- to reduce the risk of those hazards causing harm to as low as reasonably practicable.
- to decide what physical fire precautions and management arrangements are necessary to ensure the safety of people in your premises if a fire does start".

The CLG guidance states that fire risk assessment should have five elements:

1. Identify any possible fire hazards. By a hazard we are specifically referring back to the fire triangle and:

   - sources of ignition;
   - sources of fuel;
   - sources of oxygen.

2. Decide who might reasonably be expected to be at risk from fire both in and around the premises. This may be workers; visitors; guests; contractors, etc. Be especially careful to identify those people who may be especially vulnerable to fire, e.g. the young, elderly, immobile; those with disabilities; lone workers; those with language difficulties, etc.

3. Evaluate, remove, reduce and protect from risk by:

   - evaluating the risk of the fire occurring;
   - evaluating the risk to people from a fire starting in the premises;
   - removing and reducing the hazards that may cause a fire;
   - removing and reducing the risks to people from a fire – issues to address here include fire detection and warning; fire-fighting; emergency escape routes; emergency lighting; signs and notices; and maintenance.

4. Record the significant findings. Plan, inform, instruct and train, including having a plan to deal with emergencies.

5. Review the assessment as and when necessary.

Fire prevention and controls

Elimination or reduction of flammable and combustible materials

Remember that, as with all other risks, you should where possible remove the (fire) hazards that you identify.

EXAMPLE
Remove a faulty electric heater.

If it is not possible to remove the hazards then reduce any risks as much as you can.

EXAMPLE
Replace direct gas heaters with radiators or keep levels of flammable material to a minimum.

If risks have been reduced as much as possible or can't be reduced in this way, then you need to consider what fire safety measures you will need to provide to protect people should a fire start.

Fire can be extinguished by removing any one of the elements of the fire triangle:

- removing the *fuel* source, e.g. turning off the gas supply on a gas hob, will quickly cause the flame to go out.
- covering the flame completely, e.g. with a fire blanket or with a layer of foam from an extinguisher, uses the available *oxygen* and denies sufficient oxygen to the area around the flame.
- cooling a fire, e.g. with water, removes *heat* from the fire and reduces it to below its ignition temperature.

Control of ignition sources

There are many possible ways to control sources of ignition:

- substituting sources of heating like open fires or gas burners with safer alternatives such as fixed convector heaters;
- correct selection and adequate maintenance of equipment, particularly electrical equipment;
- controls on hot work such as welding;
- restrictions on smoking, particularly in residential establishments.

Control of fuel sources

Levels of flammable materials used at work should be kept to a minimum. This may be packaging; stock; product or waste materials. Good housekeeping is very important. Be careful to clear up accumulations of rubbish and keep an adequate separation distance between combustibles. Always protect skips of materials from arsonists.

Extra care should be taken with flammable chemicals or materials like foams and plastics which give out particularly toxic fumes. It may be possible to replace materials and substances with less flammable alternatives, for example fire-resistant furnishings and decorations.

How flammable materials are stored should also be considered – preferably in small amounts in flameproof cabinets (in workrooms) or in dedicated flammable stores.

Ignition sources should never be near fuel sources!

Control of sources of oxygen

This is perhaps the most difficult one when it comes to considering how it can be controlled; after all, there is oxygen all around us. One thing to do is to be particularly careful of the storage and the use of any sources of "additional oxygen". This might be cylinders of oxygen in nursing homes, for example. Make sure they are not leaking, cannot be easily damaged and are not stored or used near a source of ignition.

Systems of work

The way jobs are done can increase the risk of a fire occurring. Examples of particularly risky jobs might include:

- welding and other hot work;
- using flammable chemicals like paint-spraying;
- removing petrol from a car.

It is important that safe systems of work are followed, which may possibly include formal permit-to-work systems.

Emptying petrol from the tank of a motor vehicle is an example of a job with a potentially high fire risk. What steps would you take to do the job in a safe way?

Some of the steps to make the operation safe include those below.

DO:

- Drain fuel outdoors or in a well-ventilated place.
- Use a fuel retriever to capture the fuel and vapours given off.
- Remove all sources of heat and ignition from the area.
- Use safety signs to keep people away and take fire precautions.
- Disconnect the vehicle battery before starting to drain fuel.
- Put fuel into (marked) metal containers with secure caps.
- Place containers where they cannot be knocked over.
- Use earthing straps between the vehicle and metal fuel container.
- Soak up spills immediately.

DON'T:

- Drain fuel close to a pit or drain to prevent accumulation of flammable vapours.
- Allow any hot work (welding, electrical work, etc.) while draining the fuel.
- Use any electrical equipment such as inspection lamps, mobile telephones, etc.
- Allow smoking in the area.
- Do any work on the fuel tank before all of the fuel is removed.
- Drain fuel into open-top containers.
- Store drained fuel in the workplace.
- Add drained fuel to a waste oil tank.
- Wear clothing onto which petrol (gasoline) has been spilt.[5]

Good housekeeping

This is one of the precautions that will help to prevent fires. By keeping corridors, passageways, aisles and walkways clear, you will at the same time maintain safe escape routes. Fire exits must be kept clear.

Good housekeeping will enable us to ensure that all flammable and combustible materials are properly handled and stored, and kept away from sources of heat or ignition. Waste will be prevented from building up by ensuring bins are not overfilled but regularly emptied, and the waste safely disposed of.

2. Fire detection, fire warning and fire-fighting equipment

If a fire breaks out, people need to be informed of an emergency as quickly as possible. In small buildings it may be possible to shout that an emergency has arisen or sound a hand-bell or klaxon. In most situations, however, some form of automatic fire alarm will be required, which will most likely have automatic fire detection.

The fire warning system must warn all people in the building in all circumstances. You will need to consider whether fire alarms can be heard in all parts of the building. For example, the alarm must be loud enough to wake sleeping guests in a hotel or have other features like flashing beacons in noisy areas of factories.

Fire warning systems normally consist of an electrical system which has alarm 'sounders' (the common name for sirens, bells, klaxons, etc.) and manually-operated 'call points' (the "break-glass" boxes containing the alarm buttons) on the route of escape. The UK Communities and Local Government Department advises that this type of system is likely to be adequate "where all parts of the building are occupied at the same time and it is unlikely that a fire could start without somebody noticing it quickly"[4]. In more complex situations, for example multi-occupancy, where the likelihood of a fire being quickly discovered is less, automatic fire detection may be necessary.

Automatic fire detectors should be located in the most suitable positions. The main reason why they fail to operate is due to fire products not reaching the detectors because they are wrongly sited. The two main types are heat and smoke detectors.

Portable fire-fighting equipment

Equipment such as extinguishers, hoses, fire blankets, etc. is an important 'first line of defence' measure for fighting a fire. Such equipment is only designed for relatively small fires and should only be operated by people who are trained and when it is safe to do so. Tackling a fire when it has just started and is small is the best way to avoid serious consequences. The numbers of extinguishers needed and the type depend very much on the type of premises, the equipment you have and the processes you conduct. The fire classification table earlier showed you extinguisher types. They should be:

- sited in suitable locations, for example on escape routes;
- signposted; and
- regularly maintained.

Generally speaking, extinguishers should be located close to the hazard unless, for example, the hazards are located throughout the building. In this situation the extinguishers should be located on escape routes close to the fire exits.

Extinguishers are trickier to use than you may think. It is recommended that everyone is made familiar with the basic operation of all types of extinguishers on the premises. There may be fire marshals (see later) within the workplace or on some rare occasions a works volunteer fire-fighting emergency team. These people will require more detailed and regular training.

Extinguishing media

We showed you the types of fire extinguishing media earlier. Can you remember what they were?

Smoke alarm

As we saw earlier, the types of fire extinguishing media in Europe are:

Water

Wet chemical

ABC POWDER

Dry powder

Carbon dioxide

FOAM SPRAY

Foam spray

We also saw that fire extinguishers in Europe are predominantly coloured red and have a band or circle of a second colour covering between 5% and 10% of the surface area of the extinguisher, which indicates the contents. The circle or band colours used are:

WATER

CARBON DIOXIDE

POWDER

FOAM

WET CHEMICAL

Vaporising liquid extinguishers were also common at one time, but their use in Europe and other parts of the world was tightly controlled due to their environmental impact.

3. Means of escape

In the unfortunate event of a fire occurring, people must be able to escape to a 'place of safety'. The arrangements will vary depending on the type of premises. The escape route will need protecting to ensure smoke and flames do not penetrate it before people have had time to escape. Multi-storey premises or those which house people who are difficult to move, e.g. hospitals, will have more complex systems. All staff should be trained in and practise fire evacuation regularly. Some people, such as those with impaired mobility, will need help during an evacuation. Avoid evacuating via lifts unless they are specially protected 'escape lifts'.

The UK Communities and Local Government Department advises[6] that the following general rules apply:

- The escape route should be capable of taking the number of people who will need to use it.
- Generally speaking there should be more than one escape route.
- Escape routes should be kept clear at all times.
- The escape route to the place of safety should be as short as possible. Long escape routes will have to be subdivided with fire doors (see below).
- Escape routes should be illuminated by emergency lighting if there is no natural light or the building is used during the hours of darkness.
- Signs must be used, where necessary, to help people identify escape routes (exit and directional signs), find fire-fighting equipment and any emergency fire telephones.

The UK Communities and Local Government Department also advises that organisations should display notices which:

- give instructions on how to use any fire safety equipment and the actions to be taken in the event of fire; and
- give information for the fire and rescue service (e.g. location of sprinkler valves or electrical cut-off switches).

People should know where to go in the event of a fire evacuation. This is often known as an 'assembly point' and should be far enough away from the premises to provide a 'place of safety'.

Means of escape are protected and compartmentalised by fire-resisting doors ('fire doors'), which act as a barrier to the passage of smoke and flames. They should always open in the direction of travel along the escape route. They are rated by the amount of protection they give – normally the amount of time for which they will provide protection in the event of a fire (half-hour, one-hour). They are fitted with 'intumescent' strips, usually embedded in the door frame. These are materials that expand with heat to seal around the door and prevent or delay the passage of smoke and flames. Similar intumescent materials can be sprayed as foam into holes where services pass through walls, etc. to seal these in the event of fire.

4. Emergency evacuation procedures

All organisations should have adequate plans in place to deal with fires and other emergencies, should they arise. This includes fire drills, roll calls and a register of who is on the premises.

Role of fire marshals

Fire marshals/wardens normally supervise a fire evacuation and take charge of an emergency until the emergency services arrive. They will make sure the alarm has been sounded and the emergency services notified. They may fight the fire if it is safe to do so. They may make a roll call, often from the visitors register and staff signing-in records, to ensure everyone has escaped and make a search of the premises, particularly if, as in public buildings, it is not always clear who is on site. Again this should only be done if it is safe to do so.

Fire marshals should be properly trained. They can also have a role in fire risk assessment and inspections to ensure that fire precautions are being maintained.

Fire training and drills

Fire drills are part of an overall system of fire safety training which should be provided for workers. Fire drills test that fire evacuation procedures work effectively and that people know what to do in the event of a fire. The type and degree of detail of fire training will vary from organisation to organisation. As a general guide, UK Communities and Local Government guidance advises that employers should:

- provide details of the findings of the fire risk assessment;
- explain the emergency procedures;
- explain the duties and responsibilities of staff;
- conduct the training during normal working hours and repeat it periodically where appropriate;
- make the training easily understandable by staff and other people who may be present, e.g. in a language which people will understand; and
- determine how good the training was, e.g. by observation at fire drills.[6]

Shared premises

There are a number of issues associated with shared premises. We have already discussed the role of the 'responsible person'. Where premises are shared with other occupants or where there are 'common parts' of shared buildings like stairways, reception, etc., then the 'responsible person' might be a managing agent. You may also share a common system for alarm/detection. If it is not clear who is the 'responsible person' then you will need to make sure this is properly defined as soon as possible and ensure that this person carries out their duties effectively. All parties should co-operate with each other and share information on fire issues, for example:

- presence of flammables;
- co-ordinating fire drills;
- any building work which might obstruct fire exits, etc.

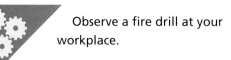

Observe a fire drill at your workplace.

How effective was it? Could any improvements be made? For example:

1. How quick was the evacuation?
2. Did the fire marshals and the other people know what to do?
3. Did people use the emergency exits?
4. Were the exits obstructed?

References

1   BS EN 13501-1:2007 *Fire classification of construction products and building elements*

2   Communities and Local Government *Fire Statistics, United Kingdom, 2007* (www.communities.gov.uk/documents/statistics/pdf/1320522.pdf)

3   www.communities.gov.uk/publications/fire/largelossfirecommercialbuildings

4   www.communities.gov.uk/documents/fire/pdf/145025.pdf

5   HSE INDG331 *Safe use of petrol in garages* (www.hse.gov.uk/pubns/indg331.pdf)

6   Communities and Local Government *Fire Safety Risk Assessment – Offices and Shops* (www.communities.gov.uk/documents/fire/pdf/151543.pdf)

Practice Questions

Q21 Which is a source of oxygen which might be present in the workplace?
A   Paper
B   Insulating materials
C   Butane gas
D   Air-conditioning units

Q22 Which is an ignition source which may be present in a workshop?
A   Hot work
B   Paint
C   Solvents
D   Waste materials

Q23 The first stage of a fire risk assessment is to
A   identify persons at risk.
B   evaluate the risk level.
C   identify the fire hazards.
D   review and monitor.

Q24 Which is NOT a suitable control measure to protect against arson in the workplace?
A   Positioning of rubbish bins/skips close to the building
B   The use of security guards
C   Control of persons entering the building
D   The use of CCTV

Q25 Which is NOT a suitable control measure for the storage of flammable liquids in the open air?
A   Storage area away from the workplace
B   Fire extinguishers located inside the workplace
C   Secure fencing and a locked gate around the storage area
D   The provision of prohibition signs for smoking and naked flames

Element 8 Hazards and controls associated with manual handling and repetitive movement

This element focuses on risks from manual handling and repetitive movements. These activities, if not properly managed, can give rise to musculo-skeletal injuries such as back pain. The UK Health and Safety Executive states that a third of all over-three-day injuries reported each year are caused by manual handling, and that musculo-skeletal injuries are the most frequent cause of work-related ill-health.

On completion of this element, you should be able to:

8.1   Identify the hazards from manual handling and repetitive physical activities

8.2   Identify ways of controlling risks from manual handling and ergonomic risks

Hazards from manual handling and repetitive activities

Before we start the main content of this element, you need to understand the meaning of some of the terms which we will use:

*   *Manual handling* is the transporting (lifting, carrying, pushing or pulling) or supporting of a load by hand or by bodily force.
*   *Musculo-skeletal injuries* relates to any injuries or diseases of the muscles of the body and skeleton together, the most common being to the back.
*   *Ergonomics* is the science of assessing the relationship between workers and their work environment. In this element we are only really interested in the assessment of musculo-skeletal risk due to the effect on individuals from the design and application of the work, tool or process. This is sometimes called 'physical ergonomics'.
*   *Display Screen Equipment (DSE)* is any equipment which uses an electronic display screen, such as a computer.

1. The scope of manual handling and repetitive physical activities

Manual and repetitive activities take place in all workplaces every day of the week. They are one of the most common activities that are undertaken at work. Unfortunately they can also present a high risk of injury. The UK Health and Safety Executive, which monitors reported injuries at work in the UK, estimates that for some industries, for example food and drink, over a third of all accidents result from manual handling. This is likely to be true in most other industrialised countries also.

The Annual Absence Management Survey by the UK Chartered Institute of Personnel and Development[1] says that in 2009 the most significant work-related cause of short-term sickness absence among manual workers was musculo-skeletal conditions, such as neck strains, strains and sprains to hands, wrists and arms, and back pain.

Back pain will affect at least one in three of us during our lifetime. For most of us this will be a short period of pain and discomfort, but for others it can be a crippling, chronic condition. It can be caused by many work situations. The exact cause is often unclear, but back pain is more common:

*   in roles that involve heavy manual labour;
*   in handling tasks in heavy industry; or
*   where manual handling is done in awkward places, e.g. in domiciliary care (support by care workers for people in their own home).

Other risk factors are related to repetitive tasks:

*   driving and sitting for long periods;
*   work which involves stooping, bending and crouching, twisting, stretching or reaching; and/or
*   excessive physical exertion, especially when tired.

Generally, back conditions tend to become more prevalent with age.

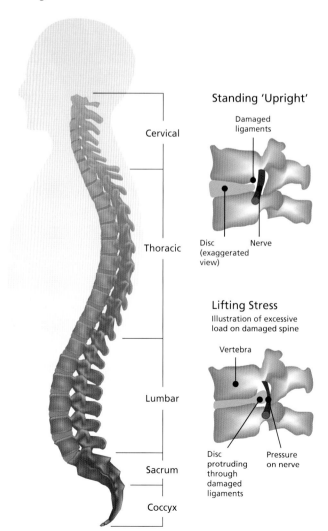

Standing 'Upright'

Cervical

Thoracic

Lumbar

Sacrum

Coccyx

Damaged ligaments

Disc (exaggerated view)   Nerve

Lifting Stress
Illustration of excessive load on damaged spine

Vertebra

Disc protruding through damaged ligaments   Pressure on nerve

Work-related upper limb disorders, sometimes known as WRULDs, affect the arms, wrists, hands and shoulders. They are most associated with keyboard use or component assembly work. Such injuries are associated with awkward, repetitive movements (i.e. repeated once every couple of minutes or so and often more frequently), particularly if they involve excessive force. Here you are often using the same muscle groups, in the same way over and over again. The symptoms of WRULDs vary but typically sufferers report numbness, aches, tingling, cramps and muscle weakness. Common examples include soft-tissue disorders such as peritendinitis, and carpal tunnel syndrome. Most people will recover if the problem is spotted early, treated, and steps are taken to control the risk.[2]

The UK Health and Safety Executive publishes information on the incidence of musculo-skeletal disorders in different jobs. It states that they are highest in agriculture, health and social care, and skilled construction and building trades.[3] The sort of activities which commonly involve manual handling and/or repetitive physical activities where there has been a high incidence of musculo-skeletal injury include:

- keyboard operation;
- assembly of small components;
- moving people;
- handling animals and crops;
- the packing and unpacking of items;
- construction activities such as bricklaying; and
- checkout activities in supermarkets.

Let us take some of these occupations and look in a little more detail at the risks.

Display screen equipment operation

Consider how you or other people work when using a computer screen.

What musculo-skeletal issues might arise? List some of the risk factors.

Operators of display screen equipment have been found to report pain and discomfort in the hands, arms, shoulders, back and neck, as well as eye fatigue and headaches.

Risk factors include:

- screen glare;
- poor image quality;
- poor lighting;
- pace of work too fast;
- reading the screen for long periods without a break;
- poor posture;
- poor or unadjusted seating;
- over-reaching;
- using excessive force on the keyboard;
- not having screen or work that you are typing at a comfortable height;
- not enough leg room;
- using the mouse excessively.[4]

Remember that workers should be encouraged to report any signs or symptoms early before they become too serious, and seek medical help if necessary. You should act on these reports to identify whether further action is needed to control the risk.

Assembly of small components

The assembly of items which requires the operative to manipulate small components, often with precise gripping with the fingers and twisting of the wrist, can result in cramps and inflammation of the muscles involved. This can be made worse on assembly lines where the speed and repetition of the actions aggravates the condition.

Packing

Packing on a production line involves continuous and often exaggerated movement. It might involve turning, reaching and stretching to select the contents, placing them in the correct position in the box with leaning over and bending, and then sealing the box. This will involve more turning and stretching to pick up the tape dispenser. The completed package might then be lifted and placed on a conveyor belt.

Bricklaying

Construction as a whole is an industry with a high prevalence of musculo-skeletal disorders. Bricklaying is strenuous and the UK Health and Safety Executive has found that there is high risk of musculo-skeletal injury particularly to the low back and wrists. This is often associated with handling of heavy materials. The Health and Safety Executive states that this is due to "issues of lack of space, poor work planning, variation in height and working in awkward postures". The weight of concrete blocks and other materials like bags of cement are also issues.[5]

Checkout activities

As items travel along a conveyor, the checkout operator will lift them and pass them across a scanner to price them. The items will then be placed down onto the packing area. This often requires a quick succession of movements, handling objects of various weights and sizes, while at the same time twisting to and from the side to pick up and put down items, and repeatedly turning the head. Often operators will lean over, over-reaching, with fragile items (such as glass bottles) and place them closer to the customer.

The way to control the risk of injury is to adopt a similar approach to dealing with other risks. If possible the risky activity, which might be carrying heavy bags of cement, should be eliminated or AVOIDED, for example by providing a mechanical lifting device. If this is not possible then a risk ASSESSMENT should be undertaken with a view to REDUCING the risk.

Remember the hierarchy:

AVOID

ASSESS

REDUCE

When a risk assessment for manual handling activities is carried out, it should be based on the most significant risk factors. These can be grouped as:

- task;
- load;
- work environment; and
- individual worker.

There are similar risk factors for repetitive actions but they are grouped slightly differently:

- task – specifically the repetition, working posture and duration of exposure;
- force;
- individual worker;
- work environment and psycho-social factors.

It is convenient to split the factors up like this, but bear in mind that they are all likely to also have an effect on each other. You should also assess whether other factors may be significant too, for example personal protective equipment. This is discussed in more detail below and we will refer back to the examples of bricklaying and keyboard use which we introduced earlier.

Assembly of small components

Hazards from manual handling and repetitive activities

Remember:

- The *task* relates to how the job is actually carried out.
- The *load* is the object being moved.
- The *individual* is anything which relates to the capability of the person or persons who are undertaking the task.
- The *environment* relates to anything specific to the working environment which might affect the task.
- *Force* generally relates to repetitive activities and is the force exerted on the body when undertaking the task. It may relate to heavy objects, fast movements or those requiring significant force, impact, compression or stress on the limbs, e.g. through a significant period of hammering nails or using a pair of pliers. It may be applied to all parts of the musculo-skeletal system (the muscles, tendons, ligaments, nerves and joints).
- *Psycho-social factors* can at first be difficult to understand as they relate to how a specific individual might react to their work, e.g. to monotonous tasks with little control; excessive pressure or demands of work; social isolation, etc.

Consider a manual handling activity that you or other people carry out at work.

What are the risk factors associated with the task, the load, the individual and the environment?

Below are some of the things you might have thought of.[6,7]

Task

- Task layout, e.g. holding loads away from the body; twisting, stooping or reaching upwards; sudden lowering movements; strenuous pushing or pulling; positioning load precisely; long carrying distances, etc.
- Work routine, e.g. repetitive handling; tasks need to be done quickly; insufficient rest or recovery time; a work rate imposed by a process.

Load

Heavy, bulky or unwieldy; difficult to grasp and hold; unstable, unbalanced or likely to move; unpredictable (e.g. animals); harmful (e.g. sharp or hot); awkwardly stacked; too large for the handler to see over the load.

Individual

Does the task require unusual capability, e.g. above-average strength or agility? Is there a specific danger to those with a health problem or a disability or to pregnant women?

Environment

Dark, cold/hot; damp; constrained; windy; bumpy or sudden changes of level; involves stairs; constraints from PPE or clothing.

Consider a repetitive task which you or other people carry out at work.

What are the risk factors associated with the task, the force, the individual and the environment?

Below are some of the things you might have thought of.

Task

- Repetition, e.g. little opportunity for change of activities; prolonged and rapid repetition.
- Working posture, e.g. static; awkward; working overhead; prolonged reaching, bending.
- Duration, e.g. length of time for which the task is undertaken in each shift; number of working days the task is performed; insufficient recovery time.

Force
Excessive gripping, particularly of heavy, vibrating power tools or heavy objects; impact from hammering; tools digging into hands.

Individual
Difference in competence and skills; difference in body characteristics, e.g. sizes; vulnerable group, e.g. disability, pregnant women; age and existing health.

Environment
Cold/hot; vibration; lighting; psycho-social (many and varied but include the amount of control people have; work demands; the variety of tasks that they can carry out; the skills that they can use; and the support they receive from supervisors and fellow workers).

Control measures

We have already mentioned that the first thing you should do is to avoid the hazardous activity if possible. In this section we are really addressing the issue of reducing or controlling the risk, as elimination is not feasible.

The control of these risks should be based on an ergonomic approach. The UK Health and Safety Executive describes this approach as "fitting the job to the person, rather than the person to the job"[7] and it works best if the workers themselves actively participate.

Very often the solutions needed to control risk can be very easy, cheap and straightforward. It may simply be two people sharing a load or even adjusting your chair correctly when using a keyboard. If you think that your problems are complex and wide ranging, you may benefit from talking to an ergonomist, but always involve workers who may already have devised their own ways of making their job safer and more comfortable.

Below are examples of controls that should be considered, but bear in mind that each activity should be looked at individually and these are just some of the controls that can work.

1. The means of avoiding or minimising the risks from manual handling

The task

- Provide handling aids such as cranes; lifting hoists; conveyor systems; people-handling aids like slide sheets (to re-position patients in bed), etc.
- Reduce the amount of time spent doing handling activities.
- Employ group lifting techniques.
- Improve the work layout by avoiding obstacles and minimise distance of move.
- Avoid pulling or activities which require significant physical effort.
- Try to always move the load close to the body and at mid height; avoid lifting overhead.
- If lifting in teams, ensure everyone knows how the load is to be carried and where the load will be lifted to.

The load

- Reduce the weight that has to be lifted, e.g. by splitting the load.
- Make sure the load is not unstable and try to spread the weight evenly across the load.
- Clearly mark the weight of the load on the outside of the packaging.
- Remove or avoid any sharp edges – provide gloves.

The working environment

- Avoid lifting on stairs and changes of level if possible.
- Avoid trip hazards and clear up spills.
- Avoid moving objects in cramped or awkward spaces.
- Provide proper lighting.
- Avoid extremes of temperature.
- Ensure all clothing and PPE is suitable and not restrictive.

The individual

- Assess the individual's suitability for the job. Do they have pre-existing health conditions which may be affected or made worse by the manual handling activity, or exclude them from manual handling altogether (such as spinal injuries)?
- Take extra care with young people, people with disabilities and pregnant women.

As with all risk, people should be informed about manual handling risks. They should also be trained and competent to do the work. This may include the need to provide manual handling training, which should always be given by a competent trainer. Training is no substitute for proper risk reduction, as discussed above. There is no weight which has been set as being too heavy to lift, as all persons obviously differ in capabilities and physical attributes. There is, however, guidance that shows how the characteristics of a load can change in different positions while it is being handled.

The UK Health and Safety Executive advises that manual handling training should cover:

- an outline of manual handling risk factors and how significant injuries could occur;
- how to carry out safe manual handling, including correct handling techniques;
- guidance on appropriate systems of work for the individual's tasks and environment;
- use of appropriate mechanical or non-mechanical moving aids; and
- practical work to supplement the theoretical work, which allows the trainer to identify and put right anything the trainee is not doing correctly or safely.[6]

Let us look at the example of bricklaying we talked about earlier and consider ways in which manual handling risks could be minimised. Specifically we will examine the laying of concrete blocks, which has been found to be a particularly high risk task. Dense concrete blocks are used throughout the building construction trade, externally and internally, often in the construction of walls. Each bricklayer can lay hundreds of blocks each day which can weigh over 20 kg each. Some examples of control measures that can be used are:

- Use mechanical means, e.g. rough terrain fork-lift or telescopic handler to deliver materials to the point of use.
- Organise scaffolding to make block laying easier, for example by providing tables on which to stand the blocks, or "half lifts scaffolds" (a section of scaffold half the height of a normal level – again to stand the blocks on) to ensure that blocks are laid at the optimum level for the bricklayer, i.e. between waist and shoulder height, and hence minimise bending and twisting.
- Use mechanical placing aids, e.g. vacuum lifts (pneumatic hoists with sucker-attachments to pick up loads and allow easy horizontal movement and positioning).
- Use reduced weight blocks (cellular or hollow blocks).[8]

The task

- Repetition: You need to reduce the number of repetitive actions, particularly those which use the same muscle groups, and allow the operator to set his or her own pace. Consider building changes of activity into the work routine, limiting the amount of time spent on one task. Develop more interesting types of work which allow a greater degree of control by the worker and reduce monotony and repetition by automation of the process.

- Working Posture: Design working practices to avoid static or awkward posture, e.g. provide enough space in the work area, including leg room if seated, so that workers can get as close to the task as they need to. Remember that people are of different sizes and have different body shapes. You need to take this into account and design workstations that are comfortable. Consider things like variable height seating, standing platforms and workstations which allow workers to find the most comfortable working height for themselves. These also allow the height to be adjusted if objects of different or varying sizes are being worked on. Design tasks so that a variation in working posture is included. Tasks are best performed when the limbs are not over-stretching and the working position is comfortable. Arm rests should be provided where appropriate.[2,9]

- Duration: Do not spend prolonged periods undertaking a repetitive task without taking a break. Build in regular short rest breaks and regular changes of activity. Look at systems for job rotation both over the working day and throughout the whole working week.

Control measures

Using a telehandler to lift materials

Force

Where possible, reduce the force needed and the amount of time for which the force needs to be applied. Ensure that tools, particularly power tools, have enough power to carry out the task. Generally, the use of power tools will reduce the amount of force needed. If hand tools are used then ensure that they are properly designed and are easy to use. If required, provide left-handed tools where needed. Ensure tools are well-maintained, are not too heavy and are comfortable for the hands. Provide gloves to reduce impact force, but ensure that the worker still has the necessary sensitivity or feel to do the task properly. Design tasks so that the muscle groups are varied and the strongest muscle groups are used, particularly those in the legs, e.g. by use of foot pedals.

The worker

Although it may at first not be obvious, musculo-skeletal problems have been linked in part to boring and monotonous work. Generally, the greater the degree of control that the worker has, the better. Try to ensure that the worker is stimulated and there is good communication with other workers and supervisors. Manage work pressure and look for signs that workers are not coping with the amount or pace of the work. Encourage team working.

The environment

Ensure that the risk from vibrating tools is being managed. Reduce vibration through proper maintenance and selection of low vibration tools. Anti-vibration gloves may also help. Lighting should be adequate so that the detail required can be seen without getting too close to the work and adopting an awkward posture. Ensure temperature is adequate and ventilation is not too draughty.

Let us again think about how we could apply some of these control principles to the example of an activity which might give rise to upper limb disorders which we looked at earlier – keyboard use.

> Consider again how you or other people work when using a computer screen. What control measures do you think are needed?

You might have thought of:

- adjustable seating;
- footrests;
- eyesight tests;
- adjustable screen height;
- document holders;
- need to stop glare (blinds/position of screen/filter);
- regular changes of activity;
- avoid using mouse too frequently;
- clear space around workstation and clear desk policy;
- positioned in front of screen;
- sufficient leg room;
- keyboard technique (use all fingers without too much pressure);
- no flicker on screen;
- upright and comfortable posture.

References/Practice Questions

References

Practice Questions

References

1   CIPD (www.cipd.co.uk/) *Annual Absence Management Survey 2010*

2   HSE INDG171(rev1) *Aching arms (or RSI) in small businesses* (www.hse.gov.uk/pubns/indg171.pdf)

3   www.hse.gov.uk/msd/hsemsd.htm

4   HSE INDG36(rev3) *Working with VDUs* (www.hse.gov.uk/pubns/indg36.pdf)

5   HSE HSL/2001/13 *Musculoskeletal problems in bricklayers, carpenters and plasterers: Literature review and results of site visits* (www.hse.gov.uk/research/hsl_pdf/2001/hsl01-13.pdf)

6   HSE INDG143(rev2) *Getting to grips with manual handling* (www.hse.gov.uk/pubns/indg143.pdf)

7   HSE L23 (3rd ed.) *Manual Handling: Manual Handling Operations Regulations 1992 (as amended): Guidance on Regulations* (www.hse.gov.uk/pubns/priced/l23.pdf)

8   HSE INDG398 *Are you making the best use of lifting and handling aids?* (www.hse.gov.uk/pubns/indg398.pdf)

9   HSE HSG57 (3rd ed.) *Seating at work* (www.hse.gov.uk/pubns/priced/hsg57.pdf)

Q26 Which area of the spine is most likely to be injured from manual handling?
A   The lower back
B   The middle of the back
C   The neck
D   The pelvic area

Q27 Which is NOT a manual handling activity?
A   Lifting and lowering boxes
B   Pushing a trolley
C   Carrying a box
D   Operating a crane

Q28 Which is NOT part of a manual handling risk assessment?
A   Task
B   Load
C   Emergencies
D   The individual

Q29 Which is a benefit of regular breaks to workers who carry out repetitive manual handling?
A   It allows the muscles time to recover from handling activities
B   It allows the workers time to consult with their safety representative
C   It encourages workers to socialise with each other
D   It gives workers the opportunity to have a drink and a snack

Hazards and controls associated with hazardous substances

This element focuses on risks from the hazards of, and controls associated with exposure to, hazardous substances. These risks may be as a result of working with chemicals, for example as part of a work process, or may be an indirect effect of a process or device, like carbon monoxide from a faulty heater. Not all hazardous substances are chemicals though – they come in many forms including gases, dusts and even bacteria, viruses and fungi.

Learning outcomes

On completion of this element, you should be able to:

9.1 Identify the forms of, classification of and routes of entry for hazardous substances

9.2 Outline the sources of information to be considered when undertaking an assessment of the health risks from substances commonly encountered in the workplace

9.3 Identify the controls that should be used to reduce the risk of ill-health from exposure to hazardous substances

The forms and classification of hazardous substances

1. What are hazardous substances?

Hazardous substances are simply any substances which you or anyone else could be exposed to while you are working, which could cause harm to your or their health.

Below are some examples of common substances which are hazardous to health:

- Motor oil in normal usage is not classed as hazardous but, particularly when it has been used and particularly if old, it can cause skin cancer due to its impurities.
- White spirit or 'turpentine substitute' is a mixture of petroleum-based solvents that is often used to clean paint brushes. It is harmful and can affect the lungs and cause damage such as dermatitis to the skin. It has a narcotic effect and can cause dizziness and nausea. It is also flammable but this property is not one which is covered in this element. Long-term exposure has been linked to potential ill-effects on the nervous system.

When you read some of the effects that these substances can have on the body, it is easy to think that everything you use at work will harm you. This isn't true if you take sensible precautions, but employers must always make an assessment of the risks to health of any substances which are classed as 'hazardous to health'.

Most often we think of hazardous substances as dangerous chemicals that we could come into contact with, but they are in fact very many different types of substances in many different forms which we need to take into account.

2. Forms of hazardous substances

One form of a substance may be more dangerous than another form.

EXAMPLE
Working with lead

Heating lead so that it gives off lead vapour is generally more dangerous than manipulating lead when it is cold, as it gets into the body much more readily when it can be breathed in.

The main forms of hazardous substances that we will consider are solids/dusts, fumes, gases, mists, vapours, liquids and fibres.

Solids/dusts
Solids are substances where the molecules are very close together and are held in place so that they do not move around. Solids can occur as large masses or as finely divided and dispersed particles.

A *dust* is a solid particle of a substance which is heavier than air, but it can be suspended in air for a period of time. Generally, the finer the dust the more dangerous it is, as it can penetrate deep into the lungs. Examples of hazardous dusts include:

- from wood, particularly hardwood, which can cause respiratory diseases and in extreme cases cancer; and
- silica from materials like sandstone which is a particular problem in the construction, quarrying, mining and foundry industries.

Fumes
A *fume* is similar to a dust, but is generally much smaller and is generated from heating and vaporising of metal or solid chemicals such as fluxes used in soldering.

EXAMPLE
A fume is given off during welding. Its degree of harm will depend on the type of metal worked on and the concentration. The welding of stainless steel for instance has been linked to lung cancer.

Gases

A *gas* is the form of a substance at a temperature above its boiling point. The molecules of the substance are widely dispersed. Many substances exist in this state at room temperature.

EXAMPLE

Carbon monoxide is a colourless, odourless and tasteless gas that is caused by incomplete combustion. It is also toxic if breathed in and is linked to a number of deaths each year, mostly from poorly functioning heating devices such as gas fires and boilers.

Mists and vapours

A *vapour* is a substance which is close to its boiling point. Many solvents, particularly those which are used in paint spraying, readily vaporise, which increases their risks as they can then be easily breathed in.

A *mist* is similar to a vapour, but contains very small liquid droplets suspended in the vapour.

Liquids

A *liquid* is the physical state of a substance at temperatures between the melting point and the boiling point. The molecules are close together but they are able to move freely past each other so the liquid can flow. The most common liquid we are all familiar with is water. We will often come across liquid hazardous substances.

EXAMPLE

Bleach, which is diluted sodium hypochlorite, is irritating to the skin and can cause burns.

Fibres

A *fibre* is a slender and elongated solid that can be spun into thread. The most common fibres that you will be familiar with are those used to make textiles like cotton. You may also be aware of the different types of asbestos – these are also fibres. They are particularly dangerous because, if breathed in, they can lodge deep in the lungs and can cause effects such as asbestosis (a fibrotic thickening of the lung which also causes scarring and thickening of the lung tissue) and cancer.

3. Types of hazardous substances

As we saw earlier, risk from hazardous substances may result from working with some *chemicals*, for example as part of a work process like paint spraying with a solvent-based paint. Alternatively it may be an indirect effect of a process or device. Not all hazardous substances are chemicals though – they come in many forms including *inert dusts* (physical irritants but not chemically harmful) and even *biological* organisms like bacteria, viruses and fungi.

Poor practice in working with wood

9.1 The forms and classification of hazardous substances

What hazardous substances are there at your workplace? Look around it and see if you can identify at least 10 hazardous substances to which you or other people may be exposed.

You can use the table below to list the hazardous substances. Try to include also the process or task leading to exposure, the form in which the hazardous substance is found and its type.

SUBSTANCE	PROCESS/TASK	FORM (SOLIDS/DUSTS, FUMES, GASES, MISTS, VAPOURS, LIQUIDS AND FIBRES)	TYPE (CHEMICAL, BIOLOGICAL)

We now need to consider the ways in which hazardous substances can get into the body. This is often called "routes of entry". Sometimes a hazardous substance can have a greater or lesser effect on an individual, depending on the nature of the exposure and the route of entry into the body.

The four main routes of entry are *inhalation*, *ingestion*, *absorption*, and *injection*.

Inhalation

This is where a substance is breathed in through the nose and mouth and passes down into the lungs. This is the most common and likely to be the most significant route of entry into the body. Once inside the lungs, hazardous substances are easily absorbed and transferred to the blood stream. They can then easily travel round the body in the blood stream and cause damage to the body's organs.

Ingestion

This is where a solid substance is taken in through the mouth and swallowed. Accidental ingestion during eating or smoking is the most frequent occurrence.

EXAMPLE

Roof workers in the construction industry may handle and manipulate solid rolls of lead. When lead has been exposed to the air for a length of time, it forms a coating of white lead oxide. This lead oxide dust can be ingested if the worker eats, drinks, smokes or bites their nails without washing after handling the lead.

Absorption

Many substances can be absorbed through both intact and damaged skin and particularly through the eyes and mucous membranes. Common examples of substances which can enter the body by absorption include pesticides and organic solvents such as petrol.

Injection

This is the least common route of entry where the substance is physically transferred through the skin. It is often associated with risks from biological organisms, for example:

- tetanus bacteria entering open wounds, from cuts on dirty objects and plant thorns, etc.; or
- hypodermic needles disposed of carelessly.

In order for us to more easily recognise the hazards associated with hazardous substances and chemicals in particular, a system of classification has been developed for materials which are classed as dangerous for supply. This classification allows us more easily to determine what precautions we should take when we are exposed to such materials.

A series of pictorial symbols (pictograms) are used to illustrate the hazard. These symbols appear on the labelling/packaging of chemicals and on material safety data sheets which give additional information on the necessary precautions. The system operates across Europe. A new system, the Classification, Labelling and Packaging Regulation (CLP), is currently being introduced so that the UK uses the same internationally agreed classification and labelling system which has been developed by the United Nations. The new system replaces the current system which is known as the Chemicals (Hazard Information and Packaging for Supply) Regulations (CHIP for short). The transition is being phased so that the new system will be fully in place by 2015. In the meantime you are likely to see examples of both systems.

Some of the more common classifications are listed on the next page. Remember that hazardous substances can be classified as having more than one hazard.

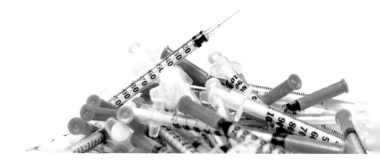

EXAMPLE OF HAZARD CATEGORY	SYMBOL	EXAMPLE OF STATEMENT
Irritant	✖	Irritating to eyes
Corrosive	(corrosive symbol)	Causes burns
Harmful	✖	Harmful by inhalation
Toxic	(skull and crossbones)	Toxic if swallowed
Highly flammable	(flame)	Highly flammable
Flammable	NO SYMBOL	Flammable
Carcinogenic	(skull and crossbones) Category 1 or 2	May cause cancer
	✖ Category 3	Limited evidence of a carcinogenic effect
Oxidising	(flame over circle)	Contact with combustible material may cause fire
Explosive	(explosion)	Risk of explosion by shock, friction, fire or other sources of ignition
Dangerous for the environment	(environment symbol)	Very toxic to aquatic organisms, may cause long-term adverse effects in the aquatic environment

CHIP Classification System

SYMBOL	EXAMPLE OF HAZARD STATEMENT	EXAMPLE OF PRECAUTIONARY STATEMENT
(exploding bomb)	Heating may cause an explosion	Keep away from heat/sparks/ open flames/ hot surfaces – no smoking
(flame)	Heating may cause a fire	Keep only in original container
(flame over circle)	May intensify fire; oxidiser	Take any precaution to avoid mixing with combustibles
(corrosion)	Causes serious eye damage	Wear eye protection
(skull and crossbones)	Toxic if swallowed	Do not eat, drink or smoke when using this product
(environment)	Toxic to the aquatic life, with long lasting effects	Avoid release to the environment
(health hazard)	*New pictogram*, reflects serious longer term health hazards such as carcinogenicity and respiratory sensitisation eg May cause allergy or asthma symptoms or breathing difficulties if inhaled	In case of inadequate ventilation, wear respiratory protection
(exclamation mark)	*New pictogram*, refers to less serious health hazards such as skin irritancy/ sensitisation and replaces the CHIP symbol ✖ eg May cause an allergic skin reaction	Contaminated work clothing should not be allowed out of the workplace
(gas cylinder)	*New pictogram*, used when the containers hold gas under pressure eg May explode when heated	None

CLP Classification System
Source: HSE INDG350(rev1) *An introduction to CHIP4*

Biological organisms are classified and labelled differently depending on how hazardous/infectious they are.

In the European Union (EU) and in many countries elsewhere in the world, suppliers of dangerous chemicals must attach a product label to the packaging and supply a material safety data sheet (MSDS) for any chemicals they supply.

1. Product labels

The label provides brief details of the dangers and precautions that you should take when handling and using dangerous chemicals. Let us look at a typical example for sulphuric acid under both the old system and new system.

Sulphuric Acid 50%

Corrosive

Causes severe burns.

Keep locked up and out of the reach of children.
In case of contact with eyes, rinse immediately with plenty of water and seek medical advice. Never add water to this product. In case of accident or if you feel unwell, seek medical advice immediately (show the label where possible).

EC Label 231-639-5

Supplied by: Amoeba Chemicals (a Unicellular Organisation),
Addison Lane, Bolsover, Derbyshire
Tel: +44 (0)1909 344 598

Example of labelling using CHIP

Sulphuric Acid 50%

Danger

EC 231-639-5
CAS 7664-93-9

Net volume: 25 Litres

Causes severe skin burns and eye damage.

Do not breathe mist. Wash hands thoroughly after handling. Wear protective gloves/clothing and eye/face protection.

IF SWALLOWED: Rinse mouth. Do NOT induce vomiting.
IF ON SKIN (or hair): Remove/Take off immediately all contaminated clothing. Rinse skin with water/shower. Wash contaminated clothing before reuse.
IF INHALED: Remove victim to fresh air and keep at rest in a position comfortable for breathing. Immediately call a POISON CENTRE or doctor/physician.
IF IN EYES: Rinse cautiously with water for several minutes. Remove contact lenses, if present and easy to do. Continue rinsing.

Store locked up.

Dispose of contents/container in accordance with local regulation.

Supplied by: Amoeba Chemicals (a Unicellular Organisation),
Addison Lane, Bolsover, Derbyshire Tel: +44 (0)1909 344 598

Example of labelling using CLP
Source: RRC Training

Sources of information

2. Material safety data sheets

The safety data sheets contain much more detailed information on the hazards presented by a particular chemical (usually a single substance), preparation or mixture (both usually blends of different substances in differing amounts). They are generally the main source of information that you would refer to in order for your company to undertake a risk assessment for hazardous chemical substances.

Safety data sheets should contain the following information:

1. Identification of the substance/mixture and of the supplying company.
2. Hazards identification.
3. Composition/information on ingredients.
4. First-aid measures.
5. Fire-fighting measures.
6. Accidental release measures.
7. Handling and storage.
8. Exposure controls/personal protection.
9. Physical and chemical properties.
10. Stability and reactivity.
11. Toxicological information.
12. Ecological information.
13. Disposal considerations.
14. Transport information.
15. Regulatory information.
16. Other information.

Hazardous substance controls

As with all of the other hazards we have looked at in previous elements, the use of hazardous substances should be avoided if possible and the risk thereby eliminated. This might be achieved by changing the work process so that the exposure to the hazardous substance no longer occurs. If exposure cannot be prevented, a risk assessment should be undertaken to determine what precautions can be taken to reduce any exposure and prevent ill-health. Generally, the greater the exposure and the more dangerous the substance, the more stringent your control measures should be.

1. Control measures

Replacing the hazardous by the less/non-hazardous

If it is not possible to avoid exposure altogether, it may be possible to replace the hazardous substance with a less hazardous or non-hazardous and intrinsically safer alternative.

EXAMPLE

Applying paint containing hazardous solvents can be made safer by changing the paint for one with less solvent, or one that is water-based.

Limiting exposure

If emissions can't be avoided, it is best to have as few workers exposed to them as possible. This might be achieved through:

- job rotation;
- limited time exposed to the risk.

Total or partial enclosure

It may be possible to enclose the process so that the hazardous substance does not escape.

EXAMPLE

A "glove box" is used in laboratories. This is a sealed container that is designed to allow the operator to manipulate objects with gloves, which are part of the construction of the box, without exposing the substance in the box to the general atmosphere.

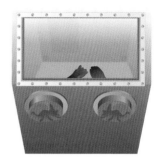

Where emissions from hazardous substances are likely to be a problem but the use of an enclosure such as that we've just described is not called for, a combination of control measures will probably be required.

Engineering control

Local exhaust ventilation should be provided, which extracts the emissions away from workers or others who may be affected. Wherever possible, the general rule should be to extract emissions of the substance near the source.[2] Local exhaust ventilation, often called LEV, consists of a collection hood or intake; some ventilation ducting; some sort of filtering or emission cleaning device such as a bag filter; a fan of sufficient power to extract the emissions effectively; and an exhaust duct normally, but not always, to the external air.

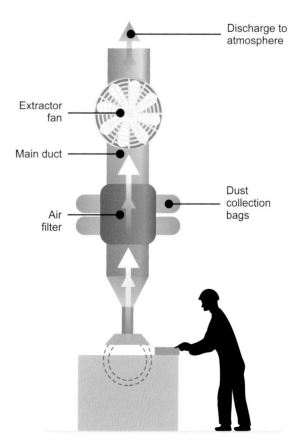

Local exhaust ventilation

Hazardous substance controls

General ventilation

Occasionally, general or dilution ventilation will be provided in the workplace to control the risks from emissions by reducing their concentration. This is often used if emissions do not occur from single points but from multiple sources such as large painted pieces (e.g. a whole door or a large table in a furniture workshop). The ventilation will often be openings or fans in the walls or ceiling of a workroom.

Safe storage

Hazardous substances should always be safely handled, stored and disposed of.

Care should be taken when handling to avoid spillages and drips of substances, especially when pouring or decanting.

Storage should ensure that:

- incompatible substances are kept apart (e.g. flammables and oxidising substances);
- flammables are kept away from sources of heat and ignition; and
- substances are in leak-proof containers in locations away from potential damage (e.g. racks being struck by fork-lift trucks).

Storage containers and locations should have appropriate labels and hazard warning signs.

Disposal must always comply with environmental legislation, to ensure the hazardous substances go to the correct disposal medium (e.g. landfill or incineration).

Safe systems of work

Safe systems of work, training, information and supervision are typical controls that organisations put in place to ensure that workers implement the controls provided to limit their exposure. This might be, for example:

- correct use and disposal of hypodermic needles;
- using a pump to transfer a liquid from one container to another rather than pouring it out; or
- correct positioning of the capture hood of the LEV.

Good personal hygiene

Good personal hygiene and the cleaning of floors, walls and other surfaces at regular intervals are likely to be important, particularly for substances which have an ingestion risk.

Personal protective equipment

As a last resort, or as a way to control residual risk (the risk that remains when all controls are in place), employers should provide Personal Protective Equipment (PPE) such as gloves, coveralls and respirators. PPE must be well maintained and fit the wearer. The worker must be trained in its use, particularly with equipment like respirators.

Information, instruction, training and supervision

The provision of adequate information, instruction, training and supervision is important to ensure work can be carried out safely.

- *Information* includes technical information (machinery manuals and material safety data sheets for chemicals).
- *Instruction* includes practical instruction, such as showing an operator what to do and allowing hands-on trials of an item of equipment.
- *Training* includes classroom theory and practical on-the-job training, often with a comprehension test at the end.
- *Supervision* is overseeing to ensure training, instruction, etc. is and remains effective. Good supervision will monitor activities and standards to determine when further training, instruction, etc. is necessary.

The role of monitoring and health surveillance

In most countries, the levels to which workers can be exposed to hazardous substances are controlled in law. These Occupational Exposure Limits are indications to levels above which workers should not be exposed. Generally, you should always aim to ensure that exposure is well below these limits if possible. *Monitoring* of workers' exposure can tell you whether you are keeping exposure below these limits and will help you tell whether your control measures are effective. Monitoring is normally done by air sampling (but not always).

Occasionally it may be necessary to undertake *health surveillance* if exposure to the hazardous substance indicates that a defined health condition could occur and early signs can be detected through health checks. Common examples might include lung function tests for occupational asthma or skin inspections for occupational dermatitis. These will be conducted under the supervision of a competent health practitioner, although supervisors and workers themselves may carry out simple visual observations which could indicate problems requiring further investigation.

2. Example of the application of control measures

Let us now look at an example of a typical, small-scale industrial process and consider the likely control measures. We will use as an example the control of dust during woodworking.

Woodworking typically generates large amounts of dust from such processes as cutting, moulding and routing. This is often as a result of working on machines, but large amounts of manual activities such as sanding can generate fine dust which is hard to control. Woodworking dust can lead to asthma and in some rare cases cancer. Hard woods are generally more dangerous than soft woods.[2]

Think about how exposure to wood dust could be reduced. You could group your suggested control measures under the following headings:

Elimination/Substitution.
Engineering Controls.
Systems of Work, Hygiene, Supervision, Training, etc.
Personal Protective Equipment.

You may have thought of the following:

- Elimination/substitution: buying sections which are cut to length; better design of product to reduce processing; minimise use of hardwood.
- Engineering controls: LEV fitted on machines, particularly moulders, belt sanders, saws, etc.
- Systems of work, hygiene, supervision, training, etc.: no large amounts of hand sanding away from LEV; put painted or varnished sections under LEV to dry; clean up regularly – vacuum not sweep; make sure LEV properly maintained; health surveillance for asthma and other respiratory conditions.
- Personal protective equipment: ensure respirators have a sufficient protection factor for likely exposure (they filter out a contaminant to a particular safe level over a set period of time).

References

1 HSE INDG136(rev4)
   Working with substances hazardous to health
   (www.hse.gov.uk/pubns/indg136.pdf)
2 HSE WIS1(rev1) *Wood dust: hazards and precautions* (www.hse.gov.uk/pubns/wis1.pdf)

Practice questions

Q30 Which is correct?
  A Ingestion of a hazardous substance is through the nose
  B Inhalation of a hazardous substance is through the mouth
  C Absorption of a hazardous substance is through the skin
  D A hazardous substance cannot enter the body through the mouth

Q31 Which is the correct description of the term "substitution" when used as a control method for hazardous substances?
  A A less toxic substance is replaced by a highly toxic substance
  B A highly toxic substance is replaced by a less toxic substance
  C An old safe system of work is replaced by a new one
  D An older worker is replaced by a younger one

Q32 Which is NOT a suitable control measure to protect workers against hazardous substances?
  A A local exhaust ventilation system
  B Enclosure of the hazardous substance
  C Portable appliance testing
  D Reduction of the workers' exposure time to the hazardous substance

Q33 For hazardous substances a manufacturer's safety data sheet contains
  A details of the range of hazardous substances manufactured by that manufacturer.
  B details of the hazardous properties of a specific substance.
  C a risk assessment that may be used by the employer who is using the substance.
  D information on the technical performance of the substance and its range of uses.

Hazards and controls associated with the working environment

This element focuses on general risks associated with the working environment. Specifically it deals with welfare and the working environment; hazards to pedestrians; psycho-social issues; noise and vibration; and first aid.

Learning outcomes

On completion of this element, you should be able to:

10.1 Identify the common welfare and work environment requirements, hazards and controls in the workplace

10.2 Identify the hazards to pedestrians in the workplace and the appropriate control measures

10.3 Identify the common psycho-social hazards which may be encountered in the workplace, the persons affected and control measures

10.4 Identify the health effects associated with exposure to noise and vibration and the appropriate control measures

10.5 Identify the requirements for, and effective provision of, first aid in the workplace

Welfare and work environmental issues

First of all, it is important to understand what is meant by the terms 'welfare' and 'working environment'.

- *Welfare* generally relates to facilities needed to ensure the general welfare of staff, including sanitary conveniences, washing facilities, drinking water, etc.

- The *working environment* is a term that is applied to general conditions which might apply at work. It includes such things as ventilation, temperature, lighting, cleanliness, working space, etc.

To ensure the health and welfare of both workers and others who may be present in the workplace, it is important that both welfare issues and the working environment are properly controlled. We will look at some of the issues in turn.

1. Welfare facilities

Drinking water

A supply of 'potable' drinking water is required. This simply refers to water which is fit to drink, which will be very easy to provide in most workplaces. However, in remote or temporary locations, as happens in the construction industry, this may be more difficult.

The amount of water needed by people will depend on factors such as temperature and the nature of the work, e.g. how strenuous it is. You do need to take care:

- that workers who may work in contaminated areas wash before they drink, to avoid any ingestion risks; and
- that the "drinkable" water is marked as such if there are other water supplies present which are not meant for drinking.

Washing facilities

Proper washing facilities are required. These should have running hot/warm water and be designed such that at least the face, hands and arms can be washed. You may have to provide showers:

- if the work is particularly dirty or strenuous; or
- where there is a potential contamination risk that you are trying to control.

Sanitary conveniences

A sufficient number of clean and well-maintained sanitary conveniences are required. As a general guide, you would normally expect to see about two toilets per 25 people, with facilities available for both sexes – usually a separate toilet or certainly a toilet cubicle in a separate room, capable of being locked from the inside. If you only employ men, the numbers can be reduced to about two per 45 workers by fitting urinals.

Accommodation for clothing, rest and eating facilities

Adequate rest facilities should be provided which are clean, dry and well-maintained and allow workers to eat meals, if they normally do so at work. Usually these facilities have at least seating and tables and should be available during rest breaks. You will generally have to take more care in ensuring that pregnant workers and nursing mothers have rest facilities close to toilets/washing facilities and where they can lie down if necessary. There should also be accommodation for clothing, especially where workers have to change into special work clothing/overalls/uniforms, etc.[1,2]

Seating

Where workers have to sit as part of their work, their workstations should be designed to be both comfortable and safe. This means that there must be:

- sufficient space;
- things such as controls within easy reach;
- seating at a comfortable height, supporting at least the lower back, and adjustable; and
- the possibility of a footrest if the feet can't easily reach the floor.

You must take special care of workstation design for people with disabilities. Workers who have to stand as part of their job should also be provided with seating to rest, and be provided with the opportunity to sit from time to time.

Ventilation

It is important that all workplaces are properly ventilated, even if there is no specific risk from airborne hazardous substances. In most cases, opening windows will be perfectly adequate. Whatever the method of ventilation, it is important that it is done with clean, fresh air. Care should be taken to ensure that any emissions, either from within the workroom or from elsewhere, are not drawn back into the work area through windows or ventilation fans.

Heating

It is important that people can work in a comfortable temperature. What this is will depend very much on:

- the type of job;
- whether it is inside or outside;
- the time of year; and
- the external climate.

In the UK generally, inside work temperatures would normally be 16 degrees Celsius, or 13 degrees Celsius if strenuous work takes place.

Lighting

Adequate levels of lighting are not only important to enable workers to perform their task properly and safely, but can also benefit psychological health. Workers will almost certainly prefer to work in natural light, although this is not always possible. Both with natural and artificial light there can be an additional problem from glare, particularly on display screens. In this case things like the positioning of the screens, blinds, etc. need to be considered.

Careful consideration also needs to be given to lighting, particularly externally, where work takes place in the hours of darkness.[2]

2. Exposure to extremes of temperature

Exposure to extremes of temperature is not only an issue of comfort, it can also be a significant health and safety risk.

Effects

Excessive cold can lead to:

- frostbite;
- hypothermia; and
- increased risk of developing health problems when exposed to vibration, e.g. from a pneumatic drill.

Excessive heat and/or exposure to the sun can lead to:

- sunburn;
- burns;
- dehydration; and
- heat stress (hyperthermia).

Heat stress can be very serious – typical symptoms to look out for include: difficulty in concentrating, muscle cramps, rash, severe thirst, fainting, exhaustion, and nausea.[3]

Some jobs, like working inside laundries or in freezers, by their very nature present risks of extreme temperatures. Both extremes of heat and cold can ultimately lead to death and workers who work in extreme climates and/or extreme conditions such as fire-fighters must be aware of the risks and necessary control measures applied. It would also be advisable to include these risks in the health screening of workers, both before and during their employment.

Welfare and work environmental issues

Control measures for heat

Examples of controls would include:

- If working internally, consider fans, ventilation, air conditioning, enclosing of heat sources, such as lagging for heating pipes, and personal protective equipment/heat-resistant clothing.
- If the work is strenuous, consider regular breaks to include drinks (particularly iso-tonic drinks – those with minerals or sugars that are easily absorbed).
- Working externally will also present problems relating to the sun. Here consider allowing for acclimatisation; ensuring that exposed skin is covered; sun block; provision of shade; and again regular rest and drink breaks.[3]

Some countries, for example in the Middle East, have set in their health and safety law maximum temperatures at or above which work must stop.

Control measures for cold

In a cold environment consider:

- personal protective equipment such as gloves and warm/insulating clothes;
- adequate local and general heating;
- providing warm workstations in cold environments like chillers;
- regular rest breaks in warmer environments; and
- easy means of escape from enclosed environments like freezers.

Effects

The health effects of smoking are well known. It has been linked to cancers, cardio-vascular diseases and respiratory diseases, notably chronic obstructive pulmonary disease (COPD). Generally, it is now not acceptable to smoke at work and in many countries, including the UK, smoking has been banned by law:

- in enclosed public places, including internal workplaces; and
- in vehicles used for work if used by more than one person or by the public, e.g. buses.

Smoking materials are a potential ignition source and also present an obvious fire and explosion hazard.

Control measures

Employers need to inform workers that smoking is not allowed in enclosed workplaces and should as a minimum display "No smoking" signs. They also need to take steps to enforce the ban and remove any existing internal "smoking rooms". These control measures should also apply to any visitors or members of the public.

An employer may consider erecting a 'smoking shelter', which should not in itself be 'virtually' enclosed or totally enclosed and should be well away from any potential fire hazards. Some employers have provided, often in partnership with health agencies, support for workers who wish to give up smoking. Many employers have banned smoking at work whether it is inside or outside buildings.

Hazards and controls for pedestrians

Accidents to pedestrians, particularly slips/trips and falls, are the most common type of workplace accident, but their seriousness is all too often overlooked even though they are very often very easy to prevent. Essential controls for all of these hazards are effective systems for information, instruction, training and supervision.

The UK Health and Safety Executive has published the following information, specific to the UK alone, which goes some way to showing how seriously employers should take slip, trip and fall hazards. Slips and trips are responsible for:

- over a third of all reported major injuries;
- 20% of 'over-3-day' injuries;
- 2 fatalities per year;
- 50% of all reported accidents to members of the public that happen in workplaces;
- costs to employers of £512 million per year (lost production and other costs);
- costs to the health service of £133 million per year; and
- more major injuries in manufacturing and in the service sectors than any other cause.[4]

Added to this, over 4,000 workers in the UK in 2009/10 suffered a major injury as a result of a fall from height, which we also looked at in Element 4.

There are other hazards which could affect pedestrians, including:

- being struck by moving, flying or falling objects, particularly from vehicles and from objects falling from overhead; and
- collision with fixed or stationary objects.

Now we will examine in more detail the most common pedestrian hazards and also look at ways in which resulting accidents can be avoided.

1. Typical hazards to pedestrians

Slips, trips and falls on the same level

Slip and trip accidents can happen for a lot of different reasons. The UK Health and Safety Executive estimates that 50% of all trip accidents are due to obstacles and poor housekeeping. Most slip accidents are due to wet conditions. Other causes include[5]:

- poor or inadequate lighting;
- sudden change of level, e.g. a ramp or steps;
- change in floor surface, e.g. from tiles to carpet;
- contamination and inadequate cleaning, e.g. oil spills;
- footwear;
- ice/snow;
- workers distracted, e.g. talking to colleagues; and
- vision obscured, e.g. carrying loads.

Such accidents also increase in the autumn and winter due to poorer light, leaves and icy conditions.

What slip, trip and fall hazards are there at your workplace? Look around it and see if you can identify at least 12 hazards of this kind. Try to group them under the following headings:

Contamination/Poor cleaning.
Obstacles (e.g. trailing cables).
Flooring (e.g. too slippery/cracked and raised).
Environment (e.g. lighting).
People (e.g. distracted).
Footwear.

Falls from a height

What do we mean by 'working at height'? Generally, this means working at "any place where a person could be injured falling from it, even if it is at or below ground level". We have already looked at ladder use in Element 4, but there are many other circumstances where people may work at height. Many of these are in the construction industry like roofwork, which we will not look at in detail in this course book. Work at height also occurs in general workplaces, for example:

- on mezzanine floors;
- at high-level openings in buildings (such as flour mills) where goods are hoisted up to and down from (so called teagle openings – see later); and
- near open cellar doors.

Workers also need to be very careful of and not tread on fragile materials where they might easily fall through. The most common example you will see is people standing on chairs in offices to reach objects.

Striking by moving, flying or falling objects

A particular danger on construction sites and in factories is the risk of being struck by a load suspended from a crane. This is made worse when the load is actually moving.

Flying objects refer to ejected materials, such as debris from a hand-held grinding machine, or pieces being chipped off stonework with a hammer and chisel. They could be parts or materials ejected from machinery as part of a process. All could strike a person walking past.

Falling objects simply refers to any objects that fall or are dropped from a height, such as a brick falling off a scaffold, or a branch cut from a tree, which could land on a person passing beneath.

Collision with fixed or stationary objects

People often collide with structures such as girders, beams, or pipework low across the ground. This is particularly the case when walking in a workplace, especially when vision may be impaired, such as when carrying something, or in poor light. In places like workshops, items of equipment may be left sticking out from a workbench and pedestrians can walk into these as they pass.

2. Control measures for pedestrian hazards

Slips, trips and falls

The UK Health and Safety Executive advises[5] that employers should consider the following controls for slip, trip and fall hazards:

- Avoid flooring that is slippery or overly polished, particularly in areas where there are sudden changes from wet to dry conditions (or the reverse), e.g. in entrance lobbies of hotels or in kitchens.
- Specify slip-resistant surfaces where necessary, particularly in wet areas, and look for signs of wear, degradation and damage.
- Suitable footwear should be provided at all times, particularly where slip risks have been identified, e.g. in kitchens, laundries, etc.
- Ensure there is sufficient lighting in work areas.
- Ensure good housekeeping and removal of obstacles.

- Ensure spills and contamination, e.g. food waste, oil, etc., are cleaned up immediately and ensure spill kits are available where needed. These are a number of items (absorbent granules, pads, leak-proof bags, sealing tape, labels, and a dustpan and brush) often contained in a bin or bag, and used to contain and collect a leaked substance.
- Put up signs warning of spills until they have been cleaned up.
- Cleaning regimes should be adequate for the type of industry that you are in. In the food industry, for example, very often steam cleaning is necessary to routinely remove grease contamination. Generally, the more likely that people are to travel over an area and the greater the likelihood of spillage and contamination, the more regular and more thorough the cleaning regime should be.
- Make sure that machines which might spill oil and other contaminants onto floors are well maintained.
- Effective drainage systems will ensure that liquids are not allowed to 'pool'.
- Introducing absorbent/anti-slip matting systems, particularly in wet areas, can be effective but they must be suitable or they can present an additional trip hazard.
- Try to avoid sudden changes of level, particularly if not obvious. If this is not possible, consider marking the floor to warn of the hazard or provide handrails.

Further controls advised by the UK Health and Safety Executive are given under "Maintenance of a safe workplace" later.

Falls from a height

The main control measure that employers should think of first is to try to avoid working at height where possible. We have already discussed in Element 4 the justification for using ladders as an example. Where avoidance is not possible, everything practicable should be done to prevent a fall and, if this is not effective, measures should be taken to reduce the consequences of a fall, e.g. reducing the distance fallen.

- Ensure that permanent work areas are fitted with suitable guardrails and toeboards with an upper rail at 900 mm or higher, and a lower rail.

- Where temporary work is taking place, consider temporary barriers, e.g. around voids or open cellar doors.
- It may also be necessary to provide workers with suitable harnesses, but always ensure that the workers are properly trained, the harnesses are secured effectively and the lanyard (the cable joining the harness to the structure) is not too long.
- In some industries, nets and airbags are used.
- Any open sides of staircases should have suitable guardrails. A handrail should be provided on at least one side of every staircase and on both sides if there is a particular risk. A centre handrail may be needed on wide staircases.

Scaffold work showing upper and lower guardrails and toeboard

10.2 Hazards and controls for pedestrians

EXAMPLE

The best control measure for high level openings is to guard the opening with suitable barriers which the worker can raise without having to approach the edge. There are also specially designed 'up and over' barriers which always present a guarded edge to the worker. These barriers allow access to an upper floor from the ground side (for instance to allow loading by a fork-lift truck) whilst guarding the high level side. They then swing up and over the load to allow access from the high level floor side whilst preventing access to the high level opening. As an alternative but less desirable option, safety harnesses could also be used with adequate handholds.

Protecting pedestrians from moving objects

We talked about this topic previously in Element 5 when we were considering transport safety. In this element we will look a little more closely at those controls which specifically protect pedestrians.

Generally, segregation of vehicles and pedestrians is always the best option. We have already mentioned general controls like signage and speed restrictions. We also mentioned earlier the marking of safe pedestrian access. These *designated walkways* assist with keeping people and vehicles apart when physical barriers cannot be put in place. They may be simple painted markings on the floor or roadway, tape barriers, or a route designated and shown by safety signs, arrows, etc.

A classic example of a designated walkway is a black and white people crossing marked on a roadway.

There are also other controls that can be employed:

- Kerbs and barriers (kerbs will ensure that vehicles do not stray into pedestrian walkways).
- Fencing and guarding to physically protect workers, particularly around doorways where people may inadvertently step out into the path of oncoming vehicles.
- Any windows, transparent or translucent surfaces or partitions should be made of safety material or be protected against breakage, e.g. fitted with wire mesh.
- Employers should also take into account environmental considerations, e.g. lighting, which can make pedestrians more difficult to notice.

PPE may be appropriate to protect people from moving objects. You read earlier about loads suspended beneath cranes – safety helmets would be appropriate in this situation. Where loads may fall from moving vehicles, high-visibility clothing would increase the chances of a person being seen by a vehicle driver. Safety footwear might be appropriate for pedestrians to prevent toe injuries.

Information, instruction, training and supervision, as in other areas, are appropriate here to ensure that both drivers of vehicles and pedestrians are aware of the hazards associated with vehicle movements, falling and moving objects. All drivers must be aware of and follow speed limit signs, give way warnings, etc., and pedestrians must keep out of reversing, loading and unloading areas. An understanding of safety signs is essential and supervision should ensure these requirements are followed.

Maintenance of a safe workplace

Employers should try to introduce regular inspections of the workplace to determine the level of housekeeping and to eliminate obvious trip and slip hazards. Regular and effective housekeeping arrangements, including the removal of obstructions like boxes and cables, will probably do more in most general workplaces to reduce slips and trips than any other control measures.

Clear leaf litter, ice and snow. Leaves, snow, frost and ice can not only be slip hazards in their own right but, like smoke and steam, can also obscure other potential hazards like steps or kerbs.

Care should be taken that doors cannot inadvertently be opened in such a way that they can injure people. In places like kitchens where access and egress is almost constant, a one-way system may need to be introduced, or doors fitted with translucent panels so that people are visible from both sides of the door.

Make sure that areas are well lit.

Noise should be controlled and, where levels are high, workers should be protected by:

- keeping them away from the source of noise (by barriers and appropriate warning signs); or
- providing them with appropriate hearing protection (ear plugs or ear muffs).

As well as high levels of noise causing hearing damage, lower levels can be distracting and stressful. You will read more about noise later.

Dust can be a common workplace hazard – either in the form of simple irritant dusts, or those from processes and materials that may be chemically harmful. All dust levels should be monitored and kept to a minimum. Simple controls can be used, such as damping down a floor or walkway before sweeping to keep dust down.

Psycho-social issues

"Psycho-social" generally relates to situations which either have an effect on or are caused by psychological or social behaviour and conditions. In this course book we are generally referring to:

- work-related violence;
- work-related stress; and
- alcohol and substance misuse.

1. Work-related violence

Persons affected

Work-related violence can occur to anyone, but is most likely to affect people who regularly deal with the public, e.g. bailiffs; police officers; healthcare staff; receptionists, etc. By violence we mean verbal aggression as well as physical violence. Violence can affect people as much mentally as it does physically. The UK Health and Safety Executive has published figures[6] from the British Crime Survey, which estimates that there were over 300,000 threats of violence and more than 320,000 physical assaults by members of the public on workers in Great Britain in 2008.

Control measures

The control methods will very much depend on the specific situation, but options to consider include developing systems of work which include effective controls to deal with:

- potentially violent clients;
- situations like lone working.

Most violent situations are born out of frustration and this can be dealt with effectively by giving customers sufficient communication. Nevertheless, violence in any form should not be tolerated by workers.

Systems of work might include:

- logging of appointments to include time and place and when workers are expected to return;
- joint visits;
- identification of potentially violent clients;
- refusal of home visits in some situations;
- not working with cash, etc.;
- a system to contact workers who work away from the central base.

Controls should also include effective training for all staff in order for them to recognise and deal with early signs of aggression. In extreme situations they should be able to use "break-away" techniques to remove themselves from potentially violent situations. Only in very extreme circumstances should workers be taught techniques like 'control and restraint'. This will apply to some workers in the health services, perhaps handling drunk or violent patients; in the leisure industry, such as door security attendants; and in secure environments like prisons.

Physical environmental controls include the design of the physical layout of the workplace. This might be associated with the seating or lighting but it should also consider things like:

- panic systems;
- coded locks;
- video surveillance;
- barriers; and
- wide counters, etc. designed to give staff more protection.

If any staff have been subject to threats or violence, this should be recorded and reported to the police if necessary. Staff must be given support to deal both physically and emotionally with the effects of violent incidents. Employers must make sure that the perpetrators are effectively dealt with, which may mean refusal of services, dismissal if a member of staff, and support for any criminal or civil legal proceedings which may be taken.

Symptoms

Stress is something that we all experience from time to time, although it is not really a health condition in its own right. It is generally characterised by mild to moderate anxiety and depression, although it can affect some people very severely and is one of the major causes of sickness absence from work.

Stress in both the short and long term can have many causes and many symptoms but in this course book we are only really talking about work-related stress; that is stress which is caused or affected by our work. The UK Health and Safety Executive says[7] that psychological stress is "The adverse reaction people have to excessive pressures or other types of demand placed on them at work". Pressure is likely to affect people in different ways and what one person thinks is stressful someone else will not. This perception of stress will depend on lots of individual factors such as the person's background, experience and importantly their health and circumstances at the time.

Control measures

The UK Health and Safety Executive has developed a number of management standards to help organisations manage stress in the workplace[8]. These standards are grouped under a number of headings, but it is important that they are seen as a 'whole system' solution to the problem.

The standards cover the following points:

- The **demands** that are placed on workers, including issues such as amount of work; speed of work; duration of 'pressure'; work patterns, etc.
- Workers who are offered **support** in terms of time, resources and physical help from managers, colleagues, mentors, etc. appear to cope better with pressure.
- The amount of **control**, independence or 'say' that individual workers are allowed in their work. Generally, it has been found that the more control workers have, the less stress they appear to suffer.
- Workers need to understand what their **role** is within an organisation. The clearer they are about this role the better.
- Organisations need to be careful that any **change** is properly planned and managed, whether it is in an individual's job role or within the organisation itself.
- Evidence suggests that a working environment which fosters positive working **relationships** in every sense is most beneficial.

3. Substance misuse

By "substance misuse" we mainly mean the misuse of alcohol and illegal drugs, but we must also take into account the misuse of solvents and legal or prescribed drugs. This is likely to be more of a problem in some countries/cultures than others, but all employers should be aware of the issues.

Signs

Signs and symptoms will vary with the substance, but general signs you can look out for are:

- mood swings;
- impaired judgment;
- poor timekeeping;
- missed deadlines/poor production;
- aggression;
- withdrawal;
- obvious signs of effects, e.g. slurred speech, drunk, 'high', smelling of alcohol, etc.;
- evidence of drug paraphernalia, empty bottles, etc.;
- increasing number of short-term, frequent absences; and
- theft.

Employers should not forget that these symptoms can also be caused by many other problems, including both physical and mental health issues.

Persons affected

The UK Health and Safety Executive has published information which estimates that alcohol may cause 3 – 5% of all absences from work in the UK, which is equivalent to 8 to 14 million lost working days in the UK each year[9].

To estimate the scale of illegal drug use in the working population is more difficult. Research undertaken by Cardiff University in the UK showed that overall, 13% of workers reported using drugs in the previous year to the study being published. Drug use was most prevalent among the young (29% aged under 30). The study also found that drug use is associated with a number of factors, particularly smoking and heavy drinking.

Even though it is a problem in its own right, substance misuse can be both a cause of and an effect of many other health and social problems such as anxiety and depression. To understand why people misuse substances is very complicated and it is important that employers, where possible, offer appropriate support to workers. This does not mean to say though that substance misuse in the workplace can be tolerated and in safety-critical occupations, e.g. train drivers, this is a major health and safety issue.

Control measures

Employers should determine whether they have a problem. This could be by looking at sickness absence records or even conducting an anonymous survey. They should then develop a clear alcohol and substance misuse policy, which should also consider the organisation's attitude to alcohol consumed during working hours, e.g. entertaining clients.

Some organisations have adopted mandatory drug and alcohol screening, but this must be done to a strict policy which is clearly communicated to all workers and contractors if appropriate. It must be very clear what the employer will do with this information and that action will follow if a worker tests positive.

Employers should encourage workers to talk to them confidentially about any problems they have. If a worker admits to having a substance misuse problem, it is far better to assist the worker in seeking help rather than dismiss them immediately. However, employers must consider that to allow workers to continue working while under the influence of drugs or alcohol could pose a very serious risk to the individual and other workers. It is also likely to be against the law to allow workers to use, supply or produce illegal substances at work.

The health effects and controls associated with noise and vibration

Noise is often described as 'unwanted sound'. Whether this sound is 'wanted' or 'unwanted' though often depends on your viewpoint. People going to a concert are likely to consider the music they hear as 'wanted sound', while to the workers at the venue or even the musicians themselves it may be simply 'noise'.

1. The effects on hearing of exposure to noise

Exposure to high levels of noise can lead to noise induced hearing loss (NIHL), which could be temporary or permanent. Early signs to look out for include:

- difficulty hearing conversations, particularly certain words;
- other people complaining that the radio or television is too loud; and
- tinnitus (the effect of ringing in the ears).

Some very loud but short noises (e.g. gunfire) can also lead to deafness.

Poor practice working with a pneumatic drill – what is missing?

What do we mean though by high levels of noise?[10] Without getting into the technicalities of noise measurement, generally:

- workers should not be exposed to continuous noise (over an 8-hour shift) of more than 80 dB without precautions being taken; and
- the higher the noise levels, the more damage that could result and the greater the levels of control required.

How do you know if your workplace is noisy? This may be obvious due to the industry you work in or the machines that you use. Certain occupations are more at risk of being exposed to high noise levels. These include:

- machine operators;
- construction workers;
- leisure industry workers (musicians, bar staff, etc.); and
- workers in bottling plants.

As an example, a quiet office is likely to reach about 40 dB, inside a tractor cab about 80 dB, and operating a chainsaw can be about 110 dB. One indication which is often used is that if you find noise intrusive and conversation difficult with people standing about 2 m away, you may well be exposed to around 80 dB. If an employer suspects that this is the case and certainly if exposure may well exceed 80 dB (averaged over 8 hours), a noise assessment should be conducted which includes noise monitoring both of the general environment and of individual workers.

2. The effects on the body of exposure to vibration

Vibration in many ways is similar to noise and many of the same issues that we have mentioned for noise apply equally to vibration.

Frequent and prolonged exposure to vibration, e.g. from power tools, can cause significant health effects. The most common conditions affect the hands and fingers and are known as *Hand Arm Vibration Syndrome (HAVS)* where the blood supply, nerves and other structures are damaged. This can be a particular problem when the hands become cold. Sufferers of these conditions in particular experience pain and numbness in the fingers, especially in cold conditions, and their fingers can appear blanched (white).

This condition is known as *vibration white finger* and in extreme conditions the lack of blood supply can lead to permanent numbness, loss of feeling and even loss of the fingers.

In recent years, attention has also focused on the effects of vibration on the whole body – *whole body vibration (WBV)*. This affects in particular drivers of off-road vehicles like dumpers, often used in construction, quarrying and agriculture. The constant jolting and jarring can lead to problems like low back pain.

As with noise, exposure to vibration should be limited.

3. Basic noise control techniques and personal hearing protection

In the UK and in many other countries, health and safety law requires employers to put in place specific controls to ensure workers are not exposed to high levels of noise. These controls should be put in place when the noise level is at and above 80 dB, averaged over an 8-hour shift.

Control techniques

Employers should generally try to eliminate noise at source or, where they can't do this, reduce it to as low a level as is reasonably practicable.

Much can be done to reduce noise by choosing work equipment such as drills which emit the least possible amount of noise. It may also be possible to redesign the work process so that noise levels are reduced, for example by limiting the amount of time in any one day or week involved in noisy activities. Companies which process small metal components can line conveyors and other systems which transport these items with rubber insulation materials to reduce metal on metal noise.

Where the general workplace is noisy, it may be possible to look at the design and layout of the workplace, workstations and rest facilities. This could include fitting noise enclosures around machines or providing insulated rest facilities, control rooms or refuges, so that workers can limit the amount of time spent in the noisy environment. It may also be possible to fit engineering controls to reduce noise. This may include silencers on machines, reducing the pressure on air lines, etc. It is also important that all machines and equipment are properly maintained, cleaned and lubricated.

Personal hearing protection

This should be provided for anyone who is exposed to noise above 80 dB averaged over an 8-hour day and should be compulsory if the noise level goes above 85 dB. These higher noise areas should be defined as 'hearing protection zones'. Workers should be given proper information about noise risks and taught how to wear hearing protection correctly.

The purpose of hearing protection is to reduce the intensity of the noise at the ear, and both ear muffs (worn over the outside of the ear) and ear plugs (worn in the outer ear) are available to do this.

Hearing protectors do have limitations. Both types offer different levels of protection in different frequency ranges (a droning sound is low frequency, a high-pitched squeal is high frequency), so an analysis of the noise should be done before specifying the type of protection to be worn. Ear muffs may offer only limited protection for spectacle wearers, and both will only give full protection if worn for all of the exposure time.

Control techniques

As we have already described with noise control, employers should always be seen to eliminate the hazard and, if that's not possible, to reduce the risk. In particular, employers should reduce the vibration exposure by trying to do the job in another way:

- without the need to use vibrating tools; or
- using tools which produce the lowest levels of vibration.

One thing that is important for HAVS is the pressure of the grip used on hand tools. Workstations that are properly designed can be effective in preventing HAVS. In particular, jigs which allow workers' arms to be comfortable and not grip the tool too tightly can be useful.

Using a jig with a hand tool

Make sure that tools:

- are working most effectively;
- are properly maintained; and
- have sufficient power to carry out the task effectively.

Specifically for WBV:

- Employers should choose vehicles designed for the terrain that can cope with the terrain that is being worked on.
- The Health and Safety Executive also advises that roadways should be as flat as possible with potholes filled and vehicles, particularly the suspension, properly maintained.
- Drivers of vehicles should be taught to drive as smoothly as the terrain will allow and they must also keep within speed limits.
- Drivers should keep the vehicle tyres correctly inflated and may also benefit from seats which have independent suspension.[11,12]

Personal protective equipment

Anti-vibration gloves have become popular. Keeping the hands warm and protected is generally a good idea, although the UK Health and Safety Executive does not advise that employers should generally rely on gloves to provide protection from vibration.[13]

There are limitations in the protection such gloves can offer. Gloves are not thought to offer the levels of protection often needed. Protection is based on certain levels of vibration, and as machinery and equipment gets older, vibration levels and patterns change, and gloves lose effectiveness in some cases. They do, as warm clothing, provide some protection to blood circulation in cold and wet weather.

Anyone who is exposed to high levels of noise should have hearing checks (audiometry) to ensure that:

- their hearing is not becoming damaged; and
- by inference, the control measures that have been introduced are proving effective.

As for noise, health surveillance looking for early signs of disease should be provided for those at risk from vibration.

First-aid requirements in the workplace

1. Role of first aid

The role of first aid can generally be seen as treatment for the purpose of preserving life and minimising the consequences of injury and illness, until help from a competent person (e.g. a doctor) is obtained.

The requirement for first aid in the workplace has been a normal part of an employer's duty for many years.

2. Types of first-aid training

An 'appointed person' takes charge of first-aid arrangements, looks after first-aid equipment and calls the emergency services if necessary.

A person trained in emergency first aid at work can give emergency first aid to someone who is injured or becomes ill while at work.

A fully trained first-aider is equipped to apply first aid to a range of specific injuries and illnesses.

Training should be provided by an appropriate organisation.

Both appointed persons and first-aiders should receive regular refresher training.

3. First-aid equipment and facilities

The UK Health and Safety Executive advises that as a minimum, first-aid provision necessary for any basic workplace should be:

- a suitably stocked first-aid box;
- an 'appointed person'; and
- information for workers about first-aid arrangements.

Workplaces may also need a specific first-aid room, particularly where there are large numbers of workers.[14]

4. The factors affecting provision of first aid

An employer may decide that the risks involved in the work mean that the appointed person does not have sufficient knowledge to deal with emergency situations. If that is the case then one or more people trained in emergency first aid at work or fully trained first-aiders will be required.

When deciding what level of first-aid provision is needed, a number of factors should be considered, including:

- the degree of risk;
- the type of substances and materials the workers use;
- the processes the workers follow;
- whether first-aid provision can cover all shift-work patterns and geographical locations; and
- what happens if first-aid staff are absent.

As a general guide in low risk environments, the UK Health and Safety Executive advises that at least one appointed person is required if the number of workers is less than 25 people. For numbers between 25 and 50 the Health and Safety Executive advises that at least one emergency first-aider should be present. If the number of workers exceeds 50 then a full first-aider trained in first aid at work should be provided for every 100 people employed.[14]

Employers are required to inform their workers of the arrangements in place for the provision of first aid. This is often achieved in consultation with safety representatives. Workers must know the location of all first-aid equipment (first-aid kits, stretchers, etc.), facilities (first-aid rooms, etc.) and who the first-aiders are. This is often done by the provision of first-aid notices that can be read and understood by all persons. Such information should also be included in induction training programmes.

Self-employed persons are obliged to make first-aid provisions for themselves.

References/Practice Questions

References

1   HSE INDG293(rev1)
    Welfare at work – Guidance for employers on welfare provisions
    (www.hse.gov.uk/pubns/indg293.pdf)

2   HSE INDG244(rev2) *Workplace health, safety and welfare – A short guide for managers*
    (www.hse.gov.uk/pubns/indg244.pdf)

3   HSE GEIS1 *Heat stress in the workplace. What you need to know as an employer*
    (www.hse.gov.uk/pubns/geis1.pdf)

4   HSE www.hse.gov.uk/slips/introduction.htm

5   HSE www.hse.gov.uk/slips/causes.htm

6   HSE www.hse.gov.uk/statistics/causdis/violence/index.htm

7   HSE www.hse.gov.uk/stress/furtheradvice/whatisstress.htm

8   HSE www.hse.gov.uk/stress/standards/index.htm

9   HSE INDG240 *Don't mix it – A guide for employers on alcohol at work*
    (www.hse.gov.uk/pubns/indg240.pdf)

10 HSE INDG362(rev1) *Noise at work – Guidance for employers on the Control of Noise at Work Regulations 2005*
    (www.hse.gov.uk/pubns/indg362.pdf)

11 HSE www.hse.gov.uk/vibration/index.htm

12 HSE INDG242(rev1)
    Control back-pain risks from whole body vibration
    (www.hse.gov.uk/pubns/indg242.pdf)

13 HSE www.hse.gov.uk/vibration/wbv/risks.htm

14 HSE INDG214(rev1) *First aid at work*
    (www.hse.gov.uk/pubns/indg214.pdf)

Practice questions

Q34 Which is an example of welfare facilities in the workplace?
A   Health and safety training
B   Risk assessments
C   Personal protective equipment (PPE)
D   Rest and eating areas

Q35 Which is an example of a slip and trip hazard in the workplace?
A   Manual handling
B   Working with hazardous substances
C   Operating a grinding machine
D   Wet floors

Q36 Which is a suitable control measure that may be used to prevent workplace violence for a worker at a petrol station at night?
A   Employ only female staff
B   Provide regular breaks
C   Improve the security of the building
D   Provide regular worker counselling

Q37 Which is a definition of noise in the workplace?
A   A measurement of sound in decibels
B   An unwanted sound
C   Pressure variations outside the range of hearing
D   Tinnitus

Q38 Which factor must an employer consider to ensure an adequate number of first-aiders are provided in the workplace?
A   The size of the organisation
B   The number of toilets available
C   The age of the first-aiders
D   The housekeeping arrangements

Workplace risk assessment activity

The following information is taken from the Guidance NEBOSH provide to students and course providers. Further information is available from the NEBOSH website, www.nebosh.org.uk.

Learning outcomes

- Demonstrate the ability to apply knowledge of the unit HSW1 syllabus, by successful completion of a risk assessment in the candidate's own workplace
- To prioritise proposed control measures and include an appropriate review date for the risk assessment

Workplace risk assessment activity

Content
This unit contains no additional syllabus content. However, completion of study for unit HSW1 is recommended in order to undertake the practical application unit HSW2.

4.2.1 Purpose and aim

- The aim of the practical application is to assess a candidate's ability to successfully complete unaided a risk assessment in their own workplace using the NEBOSH risk assessment proforma:

    - Identifying a minimum of eight hazards
    - Deciding whether they are adequately controlled
    - Where necessary, suggesting appropriate control measures
    - Prioritise proposed control measures
    - Include an appropriate review date for the risk assessment.

The time allowed to complete the assessment is not restricted but candidates should aim to complete the risk assessment in 90 minutes.

4.2.2 Marking
The practical application is marked by appropriately qualified tutors at NEBOSH-accredited course providers and is externally moderated by NEBOSH. Candidates must achieve the pass standard (60%) in unit HSW2 in order to satisfy the criteria for the qualification.

4.2.3 Assessment location
The practical application must be carried out in the candidate's own workplace. Where the candidate does not have access to a suitable workplace, the accredited course provider should be consulted to help in making arrangements for the candidate to carry out the practical application at suitable premises. Management at the premises should be consulted to ensure the candidate can carry out the risk assessment without endangering their own health and safety. Providers seeking to run the practical unit in this way should contact NEBOSH for advice and approval.

Candidates do not require supervision when carrying out the practical application, but the candidate must sign a declaration that the practical application is their own work.

Candidates, employers and internal assessors should be aware that the status of the report undertaken to fulfil the requirements of unit HSW2, is for *educational purposes only*. It *does not* constitute an assessment for the purposes of any legislation or regulations.

4.2.4 Assessment requirements
Assessment of the practical unit (HSW2) must normally take place within *14 days* of (before or after) the date of the HSW1 multiple choice paper (the 'date of the examination'). The accredited course provider must submit all candidate marks for unit HSW2 online via the NEBOSH website no later than *21 days* after the date of examination.

Any practical application result not submitted by this deadline will be declared at zero marks. The candidate will then be required to re-register (and pay the registration fee) at the next sitting date.

If a candidate is absent from the relevant written examination(s) because of illness corroborated by a doctor's note, but successfully completes the HSW2 unit within the 14 day deadline, the result will stand. If a candidate is unable to complete the HSW2 unit under similar circumstances, NEBOSH may allow it to be taken at a later date beyond the normal 14 day deadline.

4.2.5 Submission of completed work
The accredited course provider should advise the candidate of the latest date by which the completed practical application documents must be received by the accredited course provider for marking. It is the responsibility of the accredited course provider to ensure that the results of the practical application (unit HSW2) are available to NEBOSH by no later than *21 days* after the date of the examination for unit HSW1.

Candidates planning to post their submissions to the accredited course provider are reminded of the need to guard against loss in the post by sending their work by trackable delivery. Candidates are therefore advised to retain copies.

4.2.6 Further information
Further detailed information regarding the practical application unit including forms and mark schemes can be found in a separate guidance document for candidates and accredited course providers available from the NEBOSH website (www.nebosh.org.uk): *"Unit HSW2: Workplace risk assessment: Guidance and information for accredited course providers and candidates"*. Alternatively, students should contact their course provider for more information.